KETO
AIR FRYER
COOKBOOK

Publications International, Ltd.

Microwave Cooking: Microwave ovens vary in wattage. Use the cooking times as guidelines and check for doneness before adding more time.

Let's get social!

[Instagram] @Publications_International

[Facebook] @PublicationsInternational

www.pilcookbooks.com

EASY AIR-FRIED CHICKEN THIGHS (*page 72*)

CONTENTS

THE KETOGENIC DIET

This introduction is to help educate you about the types of dietary and blood fats and their contribution to health, and their relation to ketones and the ketogenic diet. Air frying tips are included on page 27. The recipes that follow focus on healthy fats, proteins and non-starchy vegetables and de-emphasize carbohydrates—particularly those that are refined or processed.

Your healthcare provider may help you determine if these approaches to eating and dieting are appropriate for you, so ask your doctor before you begin this or any other diet program.

DIETARY FATS AND OILS, WEIGHT AND HEALTH

Want to hear some good news about dietary fats and oils—especially how they relate to weight and health?

Consuming dietary fats and oils is not as bad as you might think—nor will consuming dietary fats and oils necessarily make you fat. The right amounts and types of dietary fats and oils may actually be satisfying and contribute to weight loss and weight maintenance. Dietary fats and oils are essential to your overall diet. Understanding what dietary fats and oils are and how they fit into an overall diet will help you with food selection, preparation and meal and menu planning.

The keto diet is based on ketones, organic compounds that are produced when dietary carbohydrates are limited. Ketosis is a normal metabolic process whereby the body burns stored fats instead of glucose from carbohydrates for energy. A diet based on ketosis, with its abundance of dietary fats and oils may actually help your dieting efforts.

Understanding more about ketones and their place in a ketogenic diet may assist your food choices and dietary efforts.

In addition to their role in weight loss and weight management, different types of dietary fats and oils and ketones are important for brain function, some disease protection and management, and overall health if used advantageously and correctly.

Dietary fats and oils are naturally found in foods and beverages such as dairy products, eggs, nuts, meats and seeds. Manufactured dietary fats and oils are found in some beverages, processed foods like margarine, cheeses and meats. Ketones are produced by the human body—you'll soon discover how.

There are differing viewpoints on the benefits of different types of dietary fats and oils and about ketones, the ideal amounts to consume and how ketones may sensibly be used for weight loss.

TYPES OF FATS

Saturated fats are primarily found in foods from animal sources, such as meat, poultry and full-fat dairy products, while trans fats are mostly created when oils are partially hydrogenated to improve their cooking applications and to give them a longer shelf life. Saturated and trans fats may place a person at greater risk for heart disease. On the other hand, unsaturated fats that include monounsaturated and polyunsaturated fatty acids, found in plant-based foods such as avocados, nuts and seeds and olives and olive oil, and in fatty fish such as salmon, sardines and tuna tend to lower the risk of heart issues.

The American Heart Association (AHA) Diet and Lifestyle Recommendations suggest that a person limit saturated and trans fats and replace them with monounsaturated and polyunsaturated fats. If blood cholesterol needs to be lowered, then the recommendation is to reduce saturated fat to no more than 5 to 6 percent of total calories. For someone consuming 2,000 calories a day, this is about 13 grams of saturated fat, or about 117 calories. This is the equivalent of about 1 ounce of Cheddar cheese (9.4% total fat with 6 grams of saturated fat) and about 3 ounces of regular ground beef (25% total fat with 6.1 grams of saturated fat).

Try to eliminate trans fats (fats that have been processed into saturated fats) completely, or limit them to less than 1 percent of total daily calories. On a 2,000-calorie diet, this means that fewer than 20 calories (about 2 grams) should be derived from trans fats.

In contrast, in the ketogenic diet as much as 75 percent of daily calories are derived from fat; up to 30 percent of daily calories are to come from proteins and no more than 10 percent of daily calories are to come from carbohydrates (about 20 to 50 grams).

CHOOSE THE RIGHT FATS

Fats are essential for proper body functioning and contribute satisfaction to diets, plus fats add flavor to foods and beverages. Still, fats provide more than twice the number of calories as carbohydrates or proteins (9 calories per gram compared to 4 calories per gram respectively). On a ketogenic diet, there is a different approach to fats than other diets that may restrict fats. The key is to understand the importance of fats in ketogenic diets and how to use them to your advantage.

WHAT'S INSIDE FATS AND OILS?

Fats and oils are composed of fatty acids that contain different properties. Some fatty acids are considered unhealthy and may contribute to certain diseases, while other fatty acids are considered to be healthier and may be better for weight loss and weight maintenance in the long run.

The main types of fatty acids that are found in our food supply include saturated fatty acids, monounsaturated fatty acids, polyunsaturated fatty acids, trans fatty acids, omega-3 and omega-6 fatty acids and triglycerides. Cholesterol is a waxy substance that is found in some foods and beverages and is also produced by the body.

SATURATED FATTY ACIDS (OR SATURATED FATS) are solid at room temperature. They are fully saturated or packed with fatty acids. (The name refers to its chemical makeup; saturated fats are short-chain fats with no double bonds and are "saturated" or filled with hydrogen.) They are a hard type of fat for the body to break down and may increase the risk for heart disease and stroke.

Saturated fats are mostly found in animal foods such as dairy products, lard and meats and in some tropical oils including coconut, palm and palm kernel oil. By consuming a mixture of foods and beverages that are higher in saturated fatty acids, monounsaturated fatty acids and omega-3 fatty acids, blood cholesterol levels may be lowered and blood profiles may improve. An active lifestyle is also a contributing factor in improved lipid profiles.

MONOUNSATURATED FATTY ACIDS (OR MONOUNSATURATED FATS) are liquid or soft at room temperature. They have one space or opening within their chain of fatty acids, which makes it easier for the body to metabolize or break down. Partly for this reason,

monounsaturated fats are considered to be healthier than saturated fats. Also, monounsaturated fats may help to lower blood cholesterol and decrease the risk of heart disease, so they are considered to be "heart-healthy."

Monounsaturated fats are found in avocados, canola oil, olives and nuts and their respective oils, seeds, and safflower and sunflower oils. They are more fragile than saturated fatty acids and may break down with exposure to air or heat.

POLYUNSATURATED FATTY ACIDS (OR POLYUNSATURATED FATS) may also be liquid or soft at room temperature, but they may solidify when chilled. Polyunsaturated fats have many spaces or openings within their chain of fatty acids, which makes them much easier for the body to process (and to breakdown with exposure to air or heat).

Polyunsaturated fats provide nutrients for the development and maintenance of healthy body cells, which include vitamin E, an important antioxidant that protects the cells from damage. Polyunsaturated fats may also help to reduce blood cholesterol and lower the risk of heart disease and stroke when they are consumed in moderation and when they replace saturated and trans fats in the diet. Daily fat consumption should be comprised mostly of monounsaturated or polyunsaturated fats.

Oils with polyunsaturated fats include corn, olive, soybean and sunflower oils.

Polyunsaturated fats may also be found in fatty fish including herring, mackerel, salmon and trout, along with other seafood, nuts and seeds. By reducing highly processed carbohydrate-containing foods in the diet, some polyunsaturated fats will be reduced, but those from healthier food sources should remain.

TRANS FATTY ACIDS (OR TRANS FATS) are fatty acids that have been processed into saturated fats. Trans fats are created by industrial methods through the process of hydrogenation, which solidifies or partially solidifies liquid vegetable oils. Trans fats, difficult for the body to process and eliminate, trigger inflammation. Consequently, trans fats are implicated in cardiovascular disease, diabetes, insulin resistance, metabolic disease and stroke.

Trans fats are commonly found in many fried foods and baked goods such as crackers, cookies, chips, French fries, pastries, pie crust and pizza dough. They also naturally occur in small amounts in some dairy products and meats.

The terms "hydrogenated" and "partially hydrogenated oils" on the Nutrition Facts Panel used to mean that foods and beverages contained trans fats. In 2015, the U.S. Food and Drug Administration (FDA) determined that partially hydrogenated oils (the primary dietary source of artificial trans fats in processed foods) are "generally not recognized as safe in human food." Food manufacturers were given 3 years

(until 2018) to comply with removing all trans fats from food.

Inspect nutrition labels to make sure you're avoiding all trans fats. Even if a food package states "0 grams of trans fats," it might still contain some trans fats if the amount per serving is less than 0.5 grams, so check the ingredients to make sure there are no hydrogenated or partially hydrogenated oils listed.

Omega-3 and **Omega-6 Fatty Acids** are both types of polyunsaturated fats with unique properties.

PROSCIUTTO-WRAPPED ASPARAGUS WITH GARLIC MAYONNAISE (*page 54*)

OMEGA-3 FATTY ACIDS (OR OMEGA-3 FATS) are essential fats, which means that they must be supplied by the diet for healthy body functioning. Omega-3 fats, particularly EPA and DHA, are beneficial to the heart. They may decrease arrhythmias (abnormal heartbeats) and triglycerides stored in fat cells, increase tissue flexibility, improve cholesterol profiles, lower blood pressure, reduce inflammation and slow the growth of plaque in the arteries. (Plaque is a hard substance that is composed of cholesterol, calcium and clotting materials.)

Omega-3 fats may also help to relieve the symptoms of chronic diseases such as arthritis, depression and dementia. EPA and DHA are components of hormones that regulate immune function, and DHA is vital for brain development and cognition.

Good sources of omega-3 fats include seafood such as mackerel, sardines, salmon, tuna and shellfish and plant sources like canola and soybean oils, flaxseed and walnuts.

OMEGA-6 FATTY ACIDS (OR OMEGA-6 FATS) are also polyunsaturated fats and essential fatty acids. Omega-6 fats perform vital roles in brain function, normal development and growth. They also help maintain reproduction, regulate metabolism and support healthy skin and hair and bone health. However, omega-6 fatty acids may promote inflammation and contribute to complex regional pain syndrome. Chronic inflammation may contribute to asthma, autoimmunity and neurodegenerative diseases, cancers and coronary heart disease.

Omega-6 fats are prevalent in eggs, meats, poultry, salad dressings and corn, grapeseed and sunflower oils. Linoleic acid (LA) is found in corn, cottonseed, safflower, soybean and sunflower oils among other oils. Arachidonic acid (AA) is found in small amounts in eggs, meats and poultry. LA can be converted to AA in the body. Omega-6 fats are often used in fried and processed foods, so a diet that is filled with highly processed foods may be disproportionately high in omega-6 fatty acids.

A healthy diet contains a balance of omega-3 and omega-6 fatty acids (or a ratio of 1:1), although the typical American diet tends to contain more omega-6 fatty acids than omega-3 fatty acids. Consuming more omega-3 fats through food sources, such as fish and chia or flax seeds, may help to balance this pattern.

CHOLESTEROL is an essential component in the cell membranes of brain and nerve cells and for hormone formation. It is used to maintain brain health for memory formation and for the production of hormones and vitamin D. When your skin absorbs sunlight, cholesterol within the cells is converted to vitamin D.

Cholesterol is a waxy substance that is found in animal foods such as dairy products, eggs and meats. The body produces cholesterol on its own from saturated fat or glucose so it is not needed from food.

Common thought used to be that a high level of dietary cholesterol contributed to coronary heart disease, diabetes, stroke or peripheral vascular disease. This is because excess cholesterol may form plaque between the layers of the artery walls. In turn, plaque may clog arteries, reduce their flexibility, interfere with blood circulation and lead to atherosclerosis, or "hardening" of the arteries. Plaque can also break apart and lead to blood clots. If blood clots form and block narrowed arteries, then a heart attack or stroke may occur.

Current thinking focuses more on the type of dietary and blood cholesterol and the types of fatty acids that they transport, and that consuming cholesterol doesn't necessarily lead to higher blood cholesterol levels. In fact, blood cholesterol levels may actually lower on a ketogenic diet.

LDL-CHOLESTEROL is considered to be "bad" cholesterol because it may contribute to increased plaque in arteries, decrease flexibility and raise the risk of atherosclerosis (hardening of the arteries). Excess calories, dietary cholesterol, saturated fat, trans fats and total fat in the diet are some of the dietary factors that may increase LDL-cholesterol. Lifestyle factors and genetics that may also increase LDL-cholesterol include age, diabetes, family history, high blood pressure, male gender, obesity and physical inactivity. A healthy range of LDL-cholesterol is considered to be 100-129 mg/dL. Carbohydrate consumption from refined carbohydrates that are high in sugar and low in fiber is associated with higher levels of LDL-cholesterol and

triglycerides. There is some thought that the size of LDL-particles are more important. Small and dense LDL particles may conveniently lodge in artery walls, cause inflammation and lead to heart disease.

THERE ARE TWO MAIN TYPES OF CHOLESTEROL

low-density lipoprotein (LDL) cholesterol "bad" cholesterol

high-density lipoprotein (HDL) cholesterol "good" cholesterol

HDL-CHOLESTEROL is considered to be "good" cholesterol because it helps remove cholesterol from the arteries and transport it back to the liver where it is broken down and excreted from the body. A healthy level of HDL-cholesterol (60 mg/dL or higher) may also protect against heart attack and stroke, while a low level of HDL-cholesterol (less than 40 mg/dL) may increase the risk of heart disease.

The protective benefits of HDL-cholesterol may depend upon the levels of other blood fats that are associated with coronary heart disease. For example, if LDL-cholesterol is not within normal range or if most LDL-cholesterol particles are small, even a high HDL-cholesterol level may not be protective.

Fish and soy foods, rich in mono and polyunsaturated fatty acids (MUFAs and PUFAs) may increase HDL-cholesterol. Consuming foods that are high in fiber and antioxidants from permissible ketogenic fruits and vegetables may help prevent LDL-cholesterol from injuring the artery walls.

TRIGLYCERIDES are the main form of fat that is found in food and within the body. Triglycerides are composed of three fatty acids that vary in composition (saturated, unsaturated or a combination). High levels of triglycerides in the blood are associated with atherosclerosis. Certain diseases (such as diabetes or heart disease) and medications, excessive alcohol consumption, high carbohydrate intake, obesity, physical inactivity, smoking and some genetic disorders may contribute to elevated blood triglycerides.

This is because elevated blood triglycerides are often associated with high blood cholesterol, high LDL-cholesterol and/or low HDL-cholesterol, which are high-risk factors that are associated with these diseases and conditions.

COMMON FAT-CONTAINING FOODS

Common fat-containing foods include (but are not limited to) avocados, beef, butter, cheese, chocolate, coconut, coconut milk and coconut oil, nuts and seeds (including chia and flax seeds), oils (including canola, olive and peanut oils), salmon, sardines and walnuts.

AVOCADOS

Avocados, technically a fruit, contain a lot of fat, but don't avoid them because of it! They contain omega-3 fatty acids, monounsaturated fatty acids, protein and fiber, as well as the B-vitamins, vitamin C, E and K, magnesium, potassium and healthy monounsaturated fatty acids. One cup of sliced avocado contains about 234 calories, 21 grams of total fat, 3.1 grams of saturated fat, 14 grams of monounsaturated fat and 2.7 grams of polyunsaturated fat with no cholesterol.

BEEF

Beef is more than burgers and steaks. There are three cuts: lean (3 grams of fat per ounce as round, sirloin and flank steak), medium-fat (5 grams of fat per ounce as rump roast, Porterhouse and T-bone) and high-fat (8 grams fat per ounce as USDA Prime, ribs and corned beef). Some cuts have polyunsaturated fats and others contain omega-3 fats and vitamins such as vitamins A and E, depending on their feed. Free-range beef might be rich in certain minerals from grazing. Beef is full of other nutrients, such as B-vitamins, choline, iron, protein, selenium and zinc and has prominence in ketogenic diets.

BUTTER AND MARGARINE

Butter has short-, medium- and long-chain fatty acids. The short-chain fatty acid is called butyric acid and the medium-chain fatty acid is called myristic acid. Both of these saturated fats have health benefits. They are relatively easy to transport and easy for the body to absorb. In comparison, stearic and palmitic acids, the longer-chain fatty acids, may be cardiovascular risk factors in higher amounts in the diet.

Margarine is an imitation butter spread that is manufactured from refined vegetable oil and water. Historically, vegetable oil was hardened in a process called hydrogenation that created unhealthy trans fats that contributed to heart disease. Trans fats have subsequently been removed from the majority of margarine products.

Margarine contains coloring, flavoring, milk solids, preservatives and sodium. The calories in margarine and butter may be similar in comparative portion sizes, but the composition of fatty acids differ. Generally, firmer margarines contain more saturated fats, while softer margarine may contain 10 to 20 percent saturated fats.

CHEESE

Cheese that is made from cow's milk contains about 69 percent saturated fatty acids, 24 percent monounsaturated fatty acids and 3 percent polyunsaturated fatty acids. Cheese that is made from goat's milk contains about 71 percent saturated fatty acids, 22 percent monounsaturated

fatty acids and 3 percent polyunsaturated fatty acids. Cheddar, Swiss and Parmesan cheese are some varieties with the least total carbohydrates. Use cheese to add taste, texture and healthy fats to recipes.

CHOCOLATE

The fat that is found in cocoa plants and predominant in dark chocolate is cocoa butter, which is about 33 percent monounsaturated oleic fatty acid and 33 percent stearic fatty acid. In general, stearic fatty acids from plants, although saturated, seem to neither lower high HDL-cholesterol nor increase LDL- or total cholesterol. But on a ketogenic diet, be careful about the carbohydrates in chocolate in the forms of milk solids, sugars and others.

COCONUT, COCONUT MILK AND COCONUT OIL

Coconut, coconut milk and coconut oil are used throughout the world for their distinctive tastes and textures. They were considered unhealthy due to their saturated fat content but are now valued for their healthful properties.

About 60 percent of the saturated fats in coconut oil are in the form of medium-chain triglycerides (MCTs) that are absorbed directly by the gastrointestinal tract and metabolized immediately by the liver for energy. For this and other reasons, MCTs may be beneficial in preventing atherosclerosis. MCTs may also help to trigger ketosis and may be effective for providing energy at the start of ketogenic diets.

Natural cholesterol-free coconut oil is solid at room temperature but it turns liquid at relatively low temperatures (about 80°F). It can be substituted for cholesterol-containing butter or lard in cooking and baking. Two main types of coconut oil are refined and virgin; both are acceptable for cooking and baking, but virgin coconut oil has more of a coconut flavor than refined.

There are many liquid coconut products available; they cannot generally be used interchangeably. Their carbohydrate content may be too high to include in a ketogenic diet, so check the label. Coconut milk is made by simmering shredded coconut in water and then straining out and squeezing the coconut to extract the liquid. Coconut milk beverages may act as milk substitutes. Coconut water is the liquid from the inside of a coconut and is sold for drinking, not cooking. Coconut cream is similar to coconut milk, but is thicker because it contains less water. Often a layer of coconut cream will separate from the milk in a can of regular coconut milk. To blend it back into the milk, shake the can before opening. Or just pour the entire contents of the can into whatever you're cooking and stir well (the heat will melt the cream back into the milk). Avoid cream of coconut; this is sweetened coconut cream and is used primarily in desserts and drinks.

NUTS AND SEEDS

Nuts and seeds range in total fat, fatty acids and other nutrients. They are filled with protein, mostly mono- and polyunsaturated fatty acids and omega-3 fatty acids, insoluble fiber, the B-vitamins and vitamin E and magnesium, manganese, phosphorus and zinc among other nutrients.

The fatty acids in almonds and walnuts may actually be helpful in lowering other blood fats. Almonds have been shown to help increase antioxidant vitamin E and lower blood cholesterol. Walnuts have a high percentage of omega-3 fats. Additionally, many nuts have a low Glycemic Index (GI) value, which means that they may be useful in insulin management and a good snack.

Pine nuts, common to heart-healthy Mediterranean diets, add a distinctive buttery and creamy touch to recipes. One-half cup contains about 673 calories, 10 grams of protein, 78 grams of total fat, 7 grams of saturated fat, almost 45 grams of monounsaturated fat, 24 grams of polyunsaturated fat and no cholesterol. The amount of dietary fiber ranges from 7 to 12 grams per half cup.

CHIA SEEDS

Chia seeds are tiny black seeds that contain antioxidants, calcium, carbohydrates, fats, fiber, omega-3 fatty acids and protein. Their fiber and omega-3 fat content are impressive with 11 grams of fiber per ounce (about 35 percent) and 60 percent of their total fat as ALA omega-3 fatty acids. Chia seeds are mild and nutty and add texture to foods and beverages. When mixed with water, chia seeds swell and become gel-like.

FLAX SEEDS

Similar to walnuts, flax seeds contain a significant amount of omega-3 fats such as alpha-linolenic acid (ALA): 1 tablespoon of ground flaxseed contains about 1.8 grams of omega-3 fats. Flax seeds also contain lignans with antioxidant and estrogen qualities and soluble and insoluble fibers that may offer protection against certain cancers and heart disease through their anti-inflammatory activity and heart beat normalization. Flax seeds and ground flaxseed spoil quickly so keep them in the freezer if you're not going to use them right away.

OILS

Like butter and margarine, some oils are also considered controversial—particularly the tropical oils: coconut oil, palm oil and palm kernel oil. Palm oil is an all-purpose cooking oil that is used in vegetable oil blends to impart flavor. It contains about 51 percent saturated fatty acids, 39 percent monounsaturated fatty acids and 10 percent polyunsaturated fatty acids. One tablespoon of palm oil contains about 5 grams of heart-healthy monounsaturated fatty acids.

Palm kernel oil contains 86 percent saturated fatty acids, 12 percent monounsaturated fatty acids and 2 percent polyunsaturated fatty acids. One tablespoon of palm kernel oil contains about 3.1 grams of heart-healthy monounsaturated fatty acids. Palm kernel oil is used in commercial baking since it tends to remains stable at high temperatures and can be stored longer than some other oils.

In contrast, canola oil, olive oil and peanut oil have more favorable fatty acid profiles. Canola oil contains about 6 percent saturated fatty acids, 62 percent monounsaturated fatty acids and 32 percent polyunsaturated fatty acids. One tablespoon of canola oil contains about 9 grams of heart-healthy monounsaturated fatty acids. Canola oil is commonly used for baking, frying and in salad dressings.

Olive oil contains about 14 percent saturated fatty acids, 73 percent monounsaturated fatty acids and 11 percent polyunsaturated fatty acids. One tablespoon of olive oil contains about 10 grams of heart-healthy monounsaturated fatty acids. Virgin olive oil is used as an all-purpose cooking oil and in salad dressing. Extra virgin olive oil is primarily used to dress salads, vegetables and entrées. Light and extra-light olive oil generally have less flavor and are mainly used for sautéing and stir-frying since they withstand more heat than extra virgin olive oil.

Peanut oil contains about 18 percent saturated fatty acids, 49 percent monounsaturated fatty acids and 33 percent polyunsaturated fatty acids. One tablespoon of peanut oil contains about 6 grams of heart-healthy monounsaturated fatty acids. Peanut oil has a higher smoke point than most olive oil blends, so is useful as an all-purpose oil in cooking and frying. Peanut oil is commonly used in Asian cuisine, while olive oil is used in Mediterranean cuisine. Canola oil is an all-purpose oil used in all types of cooking.

SALMON, SARDINES AND OTHER FATTY FISH

Generally the amount of omega-3 fatty acids in cold-water fatty fish, such as Albacore tuna, anchovies, Artic char, black cod, herring, salmon, sardines, mackerel and trout is significant. The amount of omega-3s may vary according to the composition of fish that fish consume, growing conditions and locations. Farmed fish may have higher levels of EPA and DHA than wild-caught fish. These considerations may affect flavor and cost.

Wild Atlantic salmon contains about 1.22 grams of DHA and 0.35 grams of EPA per 3-ounce serving. In comparison, sardines contain about 0.74 grams of DHA and 0.45 grams of EPA per 3-ounce serving and wild rainbow trout contains about 0.44 grams of DHA and 0.40 grams of EPA per 3-ounce serving.

FAT DIGESTION, ABSORPTION, METABOLISM AND STORAGE

In general, the more solidified the fat or oil, the more challenging it is for the body to process, use, eliminate or store. Monounsaturated and polyunsaturated fatty acids that are found in avocados, nuts and plant oils are largely easier for the body to handle. Saturated fats that are found in cheese, meats and milk as well as coconuts and palm products are acceptable on a ketogenic diet if consumed in moderation. Their role in cardiovascular disease is still of concern.

Avocados, beef fat, butter, mayonnaise, nut butters, poultry skin and salad dressings have delicious mouth feel due to their unique compositions of fats and oils. From the moment these buttery, creamy and smooth foods are consumed, their complex fat digestion begins.

FAT DIGESTION

Fat digestion begins in the mouth, where it is mostly physical. The teeth tear apart fatty foods and the temperature within the mouth melts some of the fats. A gland under the tongue also secretes a fat-splitting enzyme called lipase.

Then the fatty residue passes through the esophagus into the stomach, where it mixes with gastric lipase, an enzyme that is secreted by the stomach cells. Gastric lipase continues fat digestion as the stomach muscles churn and mix the stomach contents. Together, this process continues to break down the fat by breaking up large fat molecules into smaller ones and evenly distributing them.

Most of the fats in foods and beverages are packaged in the form of triglycerides, which must be broken down into fatty acids and a molecule called glycerol for absorption. This process tends to be slow. As a result, fats tend to linger in the stomach and contribute to fullness or satiety. This can take up to a few hours and is why a fatty meal is so filling and why a low-fat meal may be so unsatisfying. One of the plusses of the ketogenic diet is a lack of hunger.

Most fat digestion happens after fat passes from the stomach to the small intestine. Once the fatty residue moves inside the small intestine, the smallest fatty acids and glycerol are able to pass through the intestinal wall into the blood. They are transported to the liver where they are converted into energy and other fats as needed. Sometimes the liver stores fat, which is not a healthy condition.

The larger triglycerides are broken down in the small intestine by bile, an emulsifier that is made in the liver and stored in the gallbladder. Bile emulsifies fats by breaking them down with watery digestive secretions and prepares them for additional breakdown by enzymes. The pancreas then secretes a digestive enzyme into the small intestine, which breaks down the emulsified triglycerides even further.

FAT ABSORPTION

Fatty acids and cholesterol cannot easily travel in the blood or in the lymph, a watery body fluid that carries the products of fat digestion. This is because they are large molecules, and

fat and water do not mix (think oil and vinegar salad dressing that must be shaken before using).

To compensate, fatty acids are packaged inside a protein "shell" for their journey through the bloodstream. These protein packages are called lipoproteins, which means lipids (fats) and protein. The two most well known

SPICY LEMONY ALMOND CHICKEN (*page 88*)

types of lipoproteins are low-density lipoproteins (LDL) and high-density lipoproteins (HDL), both discussed in regards to cholesterol on page 9.

HDLs contain the most protein and the least fats and carry cholesterol to the liver for recycling or disposal, while LDLs contain mostly cholesterol. This protein to fat ratio is another reason why HDLs are considered to be "good" cholesterol and LDLs "bad" cholesterol for the body.

The fatty acids that are not used by the body are returned to the liver for recycling, disposal or storage. Excess fat in the diet may contribute to greater fat stores. But on a ketogenic diet fat is converted into energy. The majority of body cells can use fatty acids for energy when glucose is not available, except for those in the brain, eyes and red blood cells that rely upon glucose.

HALIBUT STEAKS WITH AVOCADO SALSA (*page 158*)

When carbohydrates are limited, as in the ketogenic diet, the brain can still obtain a small amount of glucose from a process called gluconeogenesis (glucose production from fats and proteins). On a ketogenic diet, the brain mainly uses ketones for one-half to three-quarters of its energy needs. This process was likely created as a survival mechanism by the body when carbohydrates were limited.

FAT METABOLISM

After dietary fats are digested and absorbed they can be channeled into energy production. Additionally, enzymes can break down stored fats to release fatty acids into the bloodstream. When these fatty acids reach the muscle cells, they go into the powerhouse of the cell, called the mitochondria.

In the mitochondria, energy is removed from the fatty acids that produce chemical energy for metabolism. Carbon dioxide and water are by-products.

Fats supply about twice the amount of calories for chemical energy production than carbohydrates or protein: 9 calories per gram for fats compared to 4 calories per gram for both carbohydrates and protein. This is why fats and oils are so calorie (and energy) dense.

Another method of fat metabolism or breakdown for energy is called ketosis. Ketosis occurs when there are little to no carbohydrates (the body's preferred energy source) in the diet. Ketosis may occur in prolonged starvation or during higher-protein diets that greatly reduce carbohydrate intake. Ketosis utilizes ketones, the by-products of stored fats, rather than carbohydrates (namely glucose) for energy.

FAT STORAGE

Fats that are not used by the body are generally stored in fat cells. Fat cells store small amounts of fat molecules when the concentration of fatty acids in the blood rises, such as after a high-fat meal or snack. An increase in fatty acids in the blood triggers an enzyme called lipase (located in fat tissue) to convert the fatty acids from the blood into a storage form within the fat cells.

The majority of stored fat in the human body is under the skin, called subcutaneous fat. A high percentage of subcutaneous fat surrounds the buttocks, breasts, hips and waist in females—likely for reproduction purposes. In males, most subcutaneous fat is found around the abdomen, buttocks and chest. There is also fat around the kidneys, liver and inside muscles. A goal in a well-designed diet program is to reduce extraneous fat— especially the fat that surrounds the organs and muscles.

METABOLISM: FATS VERSUS CARBOHYDRATES

Since the 1950's, Americans were advised to reduce fat in their diet for heart disease protection, weight loss and weight maintenance and well-being. Dietary approaches were low in fat and cholesterol and higher in carbohydrates

(starches and sugars), while higher protein and fat diets were criticized for promoting rich foods and beverages and contributing to elevated blood cholesterol.

During the 1990's when high carbohydrate diets were at their peak in popularity, obesity rates began to rise. Total calories were implicated in these increases, but also the amounts of carbohydrates in the American diet—particularly processed carbohydrates from refined breadstuffs and sugar-filled beverages— were linked with the rise in obesity.

Subsequently, new research demonstrated that low-carbohydrate, higher-fat diets actually improve HDL-cholesterol and do not significantly increase LDL-cholesterol. An examination of carbohydrate metabolism versus fat metabolism explains how this can be possible.

Your body must maintain its blood sugar within a certain range for sufficient energy to think, work, exercise and perform other activities. Insulin, a hormone produced by the pancreas, helps to shift blood sugar (glucose) into the cells for these functions.

Dietary carbohydrates in the form of starches and sugars supply your body with these needed carbohydrates. The body also has a limited store of glycogen or stored carbohydrates— about 2,500 calories—in reserve that are contained within the blood, liver and muscles. However, this amount can quickly be expended to meet the increased energy demands during disease states, exercise and fasting.

In contrast, your body has about 50,000 calories of stored fat with potential energy that can be converted into energy through a complex series of chemical reactions.

After eating or drinking, insulin moves blood sugar (glucose) into the cells for energy; blood sugar returns to normal levels and you get hungry, eat, and the process repeats. If the pancreas does not produce enough insulin (as in diabetes), this may damage the small blood vessels in the body and blindness, heart attack, infections, kidney disease, stroke or poor wound healing may result. Either oral or injected insulin may be needed—also as in diabetes.

If the body runs out of stored carbohydrates, then the liver produces ketones that can be converted into energy in ketosis (described in Fat Metabolism starting on page 16). A higher-fat lower-carb diet encourages the body to use ketosis for energy production, sparing glucose for the brain, eyes and red blood cells. This shift in energy metabolism generally results in weight loss. Depending upon the degree of ketosis, weight loss may be significant. An in-depth discussion about the ketogenic diet and dieting follows this section.

Carbohydrates contain water, so part of the initial weight loss in a higher protein and fat and lower carbohydrate diet is the decrease in water stores.

This is partially the reason why the initial weight loss at the beginning of a ketogenic diet may be significant. Another reason may be that a ketogenic diet differs significantly in food and beverage choices from a standard diet.

There may be some temporary side effects on a ketogenic diet, such as fatigue, light-headedness and/or increased urination. It is important to check first with a healthcare provider before beginning a ketogenic diet—or any diet.

Refined carbohydrates (especially those low in fat) are processed very quickly, and may first spike and then plunge blood sugar levels. Low-fat, refined carbohydrate-containing foods are also quite unsatisfying, which may backfire and cause a person to overeat. Initially the decrease in carbohydrates may be physically and emotionally discomforting, but once the body adjusts to a ketogenic state, more protein and fat in the diet may be satiating. Since fat has twice as many calories per gram as carbohydrates, you may find that you'll actually be more satisfied with less food.

THE KETOGENIC DIET AND DIETING

The ketogenic diet is hardly new. The idea that fasting could be used as a therapy to treat disease was one that ancient Greek and Indian physicians embraced. "On the Sacred Disease," an early treatise in the Hippocratic Corpus, proposed how dietary modifications could be useful in epileptic

TABLE 1
KETOGENIC DIET BASICS

Generally, the percentages of macronutrients on a ketogenic diet are as follows:

- **Fat** 60 to 75 percent of total daily calories
- **Protein** 15 to 30 percent of total daily calories
- **Carbohydrates** 5 to 10 percent of total daily calories

Both fat and protein have high priority on a ketogenic diet, with non-starchy carbohydrates completing the remaining calories. While calories are not as important on the ketogenic diet as they are for other diets, a closer examination of the contributions of these macronutrients helps to put the amounts into perspective.

If total daily calories were about 2,000, then the percentages of macronutrients on a ketogenic diet would resemble the following amounts:

- **Fat** 60 to 75 percent of total daily calories or about 1,200 to 1,500 calories
- **Protein** 15 to 30 percent of total daily calories or about 300 to 600 calories
- **Carbohydrates** 5 to 10 percent of total daily calories or about 100 to 200 calories

In selecting foods and beverages, think protein and fat first, then non-starchy carbohydrates to complete. Until you truly have a handle on what constitutes low carbohydrates, find a carbohydrate counter to help to keep you in line. The ketogenic diet meal suggestions in **TABLE 5** (page 26) may help your food and beverage selections.

---

management. Hippocrates, a Greek physician called the Father of Modern Medicine, wrote in "Epidemics" how abstinence from food and drink cured epilepsy.

In the 20th century, the first ketogenic diet became popularized in the 1920's and 1930's as a regimen for treating epilepsy and an alternative to non-mainstream fasting. It was also promoted as a means of restoring health. In 1921, the ketogenic diet was officially established when an endocrinologist noted that three water-soluble compounds were produced by the liver as a result of following a diet that was rich in fat and low in carbohydrates. The term "water diet" had been used prior to this time to describe a diet that was free of starch and sugar. This is because when carbohydrates are broken down by the body carbon dioxide and water are by-products. When newer, anticonvulsant therapies were established, the ketogenic diet was temporarily abandoned.

In the 1960's the ketogenic diet was revisited when it was noted that more ketones are produced by medium chain triglycerides (MCTs) per unit of energy than by normal dietary fats (mostly long-chain triglycerides) because MCTs are quickly transported to the liver to be metabolized. In research diets where about 60 percent of the calories came from MCT oil, more protein and up to about three times as many carbohydrates could be consumed in comparison to "classic" ketogenic diets. This is why MCT oil is included in some ketogenic diets today.

In the 1950's and 1960's many versions of the ketogenic diet were popularized as high-protein, low-carbohydrate and a quick method of weight loss. Also at this time, the risk factors of excess fat and protein in the diet were criticized for being detrimental to health. Outside of the medical community, the ketogenic diet was not widely recognized for its therapeutic benefits so response to it was sensational in scope.

Then in the 1980's the Glycemic Index (GI) of foods and beverages was revealed that accounted for the differences in the speed of digestion of different types of carbohydrates. This explanation became the springboard for a number of ketogenic diets that were revised from years earlier. By the late 1990's the low-carb craze became one of the most popular types of dieting. Since this time, the original ketogenic diet underwent many refinements and hybrid diets developed.

Variations of the ketogenic diet continued to surface throughout the

TABLE 2
ADVANTAGES AND DRAWBACKS OF KETOGENIC DIETS

ADVANTAGES

- No calorie counting or focus on portion sizes
- Initial weight loss
- After initial transition, hunger subsides
- Improved energy
- Improved blood pressure
- Improved blood fats: high-density lipoproteins, cholesterol, low-density lipoproteins, triglycerides
- Reduced blood sugar, C-reactive protein (marker of inflammation), insulin, waist circumference
- Significant short-term weight loss possible

DRAWBACKS

- Hard to sustain
- Limited food choices
- May lead to taste fatigue
- Socialization difficult
- Digestive issues (such as constipation, fatty stool, nausea)
- Nutrient deficiencies (such as calcium, vitamins A, C, D, B-vitamins, fiber, magnesium, selenium)
- Fiber, vitamin and mineral supplements suggested
- Increased urination (bladder, kidney contraindications)
- Diabetes issues
- Rapid, sizeable short-term weight loss concerning; long-term weight maintenance questionable

20th century since the premise of the ketogenic diet—higher fat and protein and low carbohydrate—was used to treat diabetes and induce weight loss among other applications.

Table 1 summarizes the basics of the ketogenic diet. Many clinical studies examined its effectiveness and safety, and advantages and drawbacks were identified (see **Table 2**).

FAT IN HEALTH AND DISEASE

Fats are essential to the diet and health for many purposes. Fats function as the body's thermostat. The layer of fat just beneath the skin helps to keep the body warm or causes it to perspire to cool.

Fat contributes to bile acids, cell membranes and steroid hormones (such as estrogen and testosterone), cushions the body from shock and helps to regulate fluid balance. Too many or too few fats in the diet may influence each of these important body functions.

One of the most important roles of fat in the body is as an energy source, especially when carbohydrates are not available from the diet or are lacking in the body. When people did manual work all day and expended the calories that they consumed, they made good use of carbohydrates and fats in their diet and within their energy stores. Today's laborsaving devices and sedentary lifestyles create less need for excess carbohydrate calories—particularly if they are refined. Even a plant-based diet

may be unnecessarily high in refined carbohydrate calories.

Over the years, as humans moved from a plant-based diet toward an animal-based diet, the composition of fatty acids in the American diet switched from monounsaturated and polyunsaturated fats to more saturated fats, which are associated more with cardiovascular disease. A diet that is only filled with saturated fats may not be healthy. By incorporating avocado, fish, nuts, oils and seeds and other foods that contain monounsaturated and polyunsaturated fats into your diet this may help to support a healthier proportion of fats in the body for weight maintenance and good health.

Besides cardiovascular disease, excess saturated and trans fats in the human diet are associated with certain cancers, cerebral vascular disease, diabetes, obesity and metabolic syndrome, which is a collection of conditions that may include abnormal cholesterol or triglyceride levels, excess body fat around the waist, high blood sugar and increased blood pressure that may increase a person's risk of diabetes, heart disease and/or stroke.

THE CHOLESTEROL CONTROVERSY

Atherosclerosis, or hardening of the arteries, is not a modern disease. Rather, the association between blood cholesterol and cardiovascular disease was recognized as far back as the 1850's.

One hundred years later in the 1950's, cholesterol and saturated fats in the diet were implicated as major risk factors for cardiovascular disease. Then in the 1980's, major US health institutions established that the process of lowering blood cholesterol (specifically LDL-cholesterol) reduces the risk of heart attacks that are caused by coronary heart disease.

Some scientists questioned this conclusion that marked the unofficial start of what's been called the "cholesterol controversy." Studies of cholesterol-lowering drugs known as statins supported the idea that reducing blood cholesterol means less mortality from heart disease. Subsequent statin studies have questioned this association. Other factors aside from dietary cholesterol have since been identified that may lead to elevated blood cholesterol, such as trans fats.

The liver manufactures cholesterol, so reducing cholesterol in the diet should help to reduce blood cholesterol, coronary heart disease and the risk of heart attack. But in some individuals, the liver produces more cholesterol than the body requires and cardiovascular disease may still develop. Accordingly, dietary cholesterol does not necessarily predict cardiovascular disease or a heart attack.

While dietary cholesterol may be a measure for greater cardiovascular risks, cardiovascular disease and heart attacks are also dependent upon such lifestyle and genetic factors as age, diet, exercise, gender, genetics, medication and stress. Reducing

hydrogenated fats, saturated fats and trans fats; incorporating mono- and polyunsaturated fats and losing weight to help better manage blood fats are other sensible measures to take.

Longer-term weight management is also a preventative measure in cardiovascular disease. Reducing cholesterol and saturated fat in the diet while integrating foods and beverages with mono- and polyunsaturated fats and oils, dietary fiber, antioxidants and other phytonutrients may lead to a decrease in overall calorie consumption and weight loss and an improvement in overall health.

SO WHAT (AND HOW) SHOULD I EAT?

If you want to lose body fat, then the general consensus is that you need to take in fewer calories than you burn for energy. For example, if you're an average woman over 40, decreasing your caloric intake may be a reasonable starting point. If you are of shorter stature and/or very inactive, or you haven't dropped any pounds after a few weeks, you may consider lowering your daily intake of calories by 100-calorie increments until you start seeing weight loss. But don't go much below 1,000 calories without your health care provider's supervision. (And be sure to check with a health care provider before making any major changes to your diet or activity level, especially if you have any health problems.)

TABLE 3
ACCEPTABLE FOODS, BEVERAGES AND INGREDIENTS FOR KETOGENIC DIETS

BEVERAGES
- Broth
- Hard liquor
- Nut milks
- Unsweetened coffee, tea
- Water

EGGS
- Egg whites
- Powdered eggs
- Whole eggs

FATS AND OILS
- Butter
- Cocoa butter
- Coconut butter, cream and oil
- Ghee
- Lard
- Oils: avocado oil, macadamia nut oil, MCT oil, olive oil and cold-pressed vegetable oils (flax, safflower, soybean)
- Mayonnaise

FISH AND SEAFOOD
- Anchovies
- Fish (catfish, cod, flounder, halibut, mackerel, mahi-mahi, salmon, snapper, trout, tuna)
- Shellfish (clams, crab, lobster, mussels, oysters, scallops, squid)

FRUITS AND VEGETABLES
- Avocados
- Cruciferous vegetables (broccoli, Brussels sprouts, cabbage, cauliflower, kohlrabi)
- Fermented vegetables (kimchi, sauerkraut)
- Leafy greens (bok choy, chard, endive, lettuce, kale, radicchio, spinach, watercress)
- Lemon and lime juice and peel
- Mushrooms
- Non-starchy vegetables (asparagus, bamboo shoots, celery, cucumber)
- Seaweed and kelp
- Squash (spaghetti squash, yellow squash, zucchini)
- Tomatoes (used in moderation in some keto diets)

DAIRY PRODUCTS
- Crème fraîche
- Greek yogurt
- Hard cheese (aged Cheddar, feta, Parmesan, Swiss)
- Heavy cream
- Soft cheese (Brie, blue, Colby, Monterey Jack, mozzarella)
- Sour cream
- Spreadable cheese (cream cheese, cottage cheese and mascarpone)

MEATS AND POULTRY
- Beef (ground beef, roasts, steak, stew meat)
- Goat (leg, loin, rack, saddle, shoulder)
- Lamb (leg, loin, rack, ribs, shank, shoulder)
- Organ meats (heart, kidneys, liver, tongue)
- Poultry with skin (such as chicken, duck, pheasant, quail, turkey)
- Pork (bacon and sausage without fillers, ground pork, ham, pork chops, pork loin, tenderloin)
- Tofu (used in moderation in some keto diets)
- Veal (double, flank, leg, rib, shoulder, sirloin)

NON-DAIRY BEVERAGES
- Almond milk
- Cashew milk
- Coconut milk
- Soymilk (used in moderation in some keto diets)

NUTS AND SEEDS
- Nut butters (almond, macadamia)
- Seeds (chia, flax, poppy, sesame, sunflower)
- Whole nuts (almonds, Brazil nuts, hazelnuts, macadamia, pecans, peanuts, pine nuts, walnuts)

PANTRY ITEMS
- Herbs (dried or fresh such as basil, cilantro, oregano, parsley, rosemary and thyme)
- Horseradish
- Hot sauce
- Mustard
- Pepper
- Pesto sauce
- Pickles
- Salad dressings (without sweeteners)
- Salt
- Spices (such as ground red pepper, chili powder, cinnamon and cumin)
- Unsweetened gelatin
- Vinegar
- Whey protein (unsweetened)
- Worcestershire sauce

The ketogenic diet is another approach to weight loss, one that does not focus on calories. Instead, it focuses on the composition of calories from fats, proteins and carbohydrates.

Fats are satisfying because they take longer for the body to digest, and some are converted into ketones for energy. You don't want to skimp on proteins because protein helps maintain and build calorie-burning muscle and also keeps you satiated between

PORK TENDERLOIN WITH AVOCADO-TOMATILLO SALSA (*page 110*)

meals. Choose protein sources that supply monounsaturated fats and other heart-healthy unsaturated fats; good options include fish, seafood, nuts and seeds. (Fatty fish, such as

herring, mackerel, salmon and tuna contain polyunsaturated fats—especially disease-fighting omega-3 fatty acids). You'll need to replace highly processed and refined foods that are full of saturated and trans fats, sugar and refined carbohydrates with minimally processed fiber- and nutrient-rich foods that include non-starchy vegetables.

What you'll likely end up with is a satisfying eating plan with ample protein, healthy fats and minimal carbohydrates that may help you to feel full and lose weight in the process. It's also a plan that may help you to maintain weight loss over time in a modified manner.

If you've ever tried to lose weight before, you know how quickly between-meal hunger may sabotage your best efforts. When your stomach starts rumbling hours before your next meal, it's tempting to grab whatever is available. Often, that "whatever" is some unhealthy packaged snack food or beverage that is loaded with empty calories, sodium, sugars and/ or unhealthy fats. Or, if you manage to ignore this hunger, you may become so ravenous at the next meal that you consume far more calories than your body actually needs.

To prevent hunger from spoiling your weight-loss efforts, eat when you are hungry and stop eating when you are full, whether a meal or snack. Try to consume meals and snacks that include a source of hunger-fighting protein and healthy fat, and count your carbs so as

TABLE 4
UNACCEPTABLE FOODS, BEVERAGES AND INGREDIENTS FOR KETOGENIC DIETS

- Alcohol other than hard liquor (beer, sugary alcoholic beverages, wine)
- Beans
- Breads and breadstuffs
- Cakes and pastries
- Candy
- Cereals
- Cookies
- Crackers
- Flours
- Fruit, all (fresh, dried)
- Grains (amaranth, barley, buckwheat, bulgur, corn, millet, oats, rice, rye, sorghum, sprouted grains, wheat)
- Legumes (lentils, peas)
- Margarines with trans fats
- Milk (some full-fat milk is acceptable in some ketogenic diets)
- Oats and muesli
- Potatoes, all kinds (white, yellow, sweet)
- Quinoa
- Pasta
- Pizza
- Processed and refined snack foods
- Rice
- Root vegetables
- Soda
- Sports drinks
- Sugar and honey
- Syrup
- Wheat gluten
- Yams

not to exceed the daily limit of 20 to 50 grams of non-starchy carbohydrates.

Drink plenty of water throughout the day (especially if you live in a hot climate or sweat excessively) since ketogenic diets tend to be dehydrating and may lead to fatigue or ill feelings. This may be due to an imbalance of electrolytes; specifically sodium that the kidneys excrete during ketosis. Sometimes lightly salting your food may help to restore sodium or taking a high-quality vitamin and mineral supplement.

NOTES ON KETOGENIC FOODS, BEVERAGES AND INGREDIENTS

In general, the foods, beverages and ingredients that are included in a ketogenic diet incorporate eggs, healthy fats and oils, fish, meats and organ meats and non-starchy vegetables. These "acceptable" foods, beverages and ingredients contain protein and fats and are low in carbohydrates that contribute to the effectiveness of ketogenic diets. They are listed in **TABLE 3 – ACCEPTABLE FOODS, BEVERAGES AND INGREDIENTS FOR KETOGENIC DIETS**.

In **TABLE 4 – UNACCEPTABLE FOODS, BEVERAGES AND INGREDIENTS FOR KETOGENIC DIETS** are shown. While there is a wide-range of ketogenic diet approaches, these foods, beverages and ingredients are generally considered to be "unacceptable" on many ketogenic diets. In general, their carbohydrate content exceeds what is considered as optimal for effective ketosis and diet success.

TABLE 5
SAMPLE KETOGENIC DIET MEALS: BREAKFAST, LUNCH, DINNER AND SNACKS

Examples of combinations of protein + low-carb, non-starchy vegetables + fats:

BREAKFAST:

- Almond, coconut, hemp or other nut or seed milks or beverages (unsweetened)
- Bacon, sausage or sliced meats (without carbohydrate fillers)
- Cheese, hard or soft varieties
- Eggs, scrambled or fried + vegetables (asparagus, broccoli, garlic, mushrooms, onions or spinach) + coconut or olive oil + avocado, olives, salsa and/or sour cream
- Greek yogurt with nut butter, chia or flax seeds, herbs and spices (cinnamon, ginger or nutmeg)
- Smoked fish (such as lox, sable or whitefish)
- Smoothies made with keto-friendly ingredients (protein powder, almond or coconut butter, avocado, cocoa powder, chia or flax seeds, spices such as cinnamon, smoked paprika or turmeric and unsweetened almond or hemp milk)
- Vegetable slices (cucumber or zucchini or lettuce) topped with cheese

LUNCH AND DINNER:

- Eggs + watercress or spinach + avocado dressing
- Lamb + kale + sesame oil
- Pork + cauliflower + coconut butter
- Poultry + zucchini and yellow squash + extra virgin olive oil
- Salmon + broccoli + mustard sauce
- Sardines + cucumbers and onions + sour cream dressing
- Seafood + leafy green salad + oil and vinegar dressing
- Steak + asparagus + butter sauce
- Tofu + mushrooms and bok choy + ghee
- Tuna + celery + mayonnaise

SNACKS:

- Asparagus with goat cheese dip
- Avocado filled hard-cooked eggs
- Celery + nut or seed butter
- Cheese + olive skewers
- Chia and flaxseed crackers + cream cheese
- Cucumber and cream cheese spread
- Cream cheese and bacon stuffed celery
- Deviled eggs with fresh herbs and chives
- Greek yogurt with chopped cucumbers and garlic
- Guacamole with onions and garlic
- Ham and Cheddar or Swiss cheese roll ups
- Mixed nut-coated cheese balls
- Nut butters (such as almond) blended with ricotta cheese
- Olives stuffed with blue cheese
- Parmesan cheese crisps
- Seeds and seed butters such as tahini
- Sliced jicama with herbed cream cheese

HELPFUL AIR FRYING TIPS

- Read your air fryer's manufacturer's directions carefully before cooking to make sure you understand the specific features of your air fryer before starting to cook.

- Preheat your air fryer for 2 to 3 minutes before cooking.

- You can cook foods typically prepared in the oven in your air fryer. But because the air fryer is more condensed than a regular oven, it is recommended that recipes cut 25°F to 50°F off temperature and 20% off the typical cooking times.

- Avoid having foods stick to your air fryer basket by using nonstick cooking spray or cooking on parchment paper or foil. You can also get food to brown and crisp more easily by spraying occasionally with nonstick cooking spray during the cooking process.

- Don't overfill your basket. Each air fryer differs in its basket size. Cook food in batches as needed.

- Use toothpicks to hold food in place. You may notice that light foods may blow around from the pressure of the fan. Just be sure to secure foods in the basket to prevent this.

- Check foods while cooking by opening the air fryer basket. This will not disturb cooking times. Once you return the basket, the cooking resumes.

- Experiment with cooking times of various foods. Test foods for doneness before consuming—check meats and poultry with a meat thermometer.

- Use your air fryer to cook frozen foods, too! Just remember to reduce cooking temperatures and times.

ESTIMATED COOKING TEMPERATURES/TIMES*

FOOD	TEMPERATURE	TIMING
Vegetables (asparagus, broccoli, corn-on-the-cob, green beans, mushrooms, cherry tomatoes)	390°F	5 to 6 min.
Vegetables (bell peppers, cauliflower, eggplant, onions, potatoes, zucchini)	390°F	8 to 12 min.
Chicken (bone-in)	370°F	20 to 25 min.
Chicken (boneless)	370°F	12 to 15 min.
Beef (ground beef)	370°F	15 to 17 min.
Beef (steaks, roasts)	390°F	10 to 15 min.
Pork	370°F	12 to 15 min.
Fish	390°F	10 to 12 min.
Frozen Foods	390°F	10 to 15 min.

This is just a guide. All food varies in size, weight, and texture. Be sure to test your food for preferred doneness before consuming it. Also, some foods will need to be shaken or flipped to help distribute ingredients for proper cooking.

Make note of the temperatures and times that work best for you for continued success of your air fryer.

APPETIZERS & SNACKS

MINI SPINACH FRITTATAS
MAKES 12 MINI FRITTATAS (4 TO 6 SERVINGS)

CALORIES
290

TOTAL
FAT
20g

CARBS
6g

NET
CARBS
4g

DIETARY
FIBER
2g

PROTEIN
21g

1 tablespoon olive oil
½ cup chopped onion
8 eggs
¼ cup plain yogurt
1 package (10 ounces) frozen chopped spinach, thawed and squeezed dry

½ cup (2 ounces) shredded white Cheddar cheese
¼ cup grated Parmesan cheese
¾ teaspoon salt
⅛ teaspoon black pepper
⅛ teaspoon ground red pepper
Pinch ground nutmeg

1 Heat oil in large skillet over medium heat. Add onion; cook and stir 5 minutes or until tender. Set aside to cool slightly.

2 Preheat air fryer to 370°F. Lightly spray 12 standard (2½-inch) silicone muffin cups with nonstick cooking spray.

3 Whisk eggs and yogurt in large bowl. Stir in spinach, Cheddar, onion, Parmesan, salt, black pepper, red pepper and nutmeg until blended. Divide mixture evenly among prepared muffin cups.

4 Cook in batches 12 to 15 minutes or until eggs are puffed, firm and no longer shiny. Cool in cups 2 minutes. Loosen bottom and sides with small spatula or knife; remove to wire rack. Serve warm, cold or at room temperature.

JALAPEÑO POPPERS
MAKES 20 TO 24 POPPERS

10 to 12 fresh jalapeño peppers*

1 package (8 ounces) cream cheese, softened

1½ cups (6 ounces) shredded Cheddar cheese, divided

2 green onions, finely chopped

½ teaspoon onion powder

¼ teaspoon salt

⅛ teaspoon garlic powder

6 slices bacon, crisp-cooked and finely chopped

2 tablespoons almond flour (optional)

2 tablespoons grated Parmesan or Romano cheese

For large jalapeño peppers, use 10. For small peppers, use 12.

1 Cut each jalapeño** in half lengthwise; remove ribs and seeds.

2 Combine cream cheese, 1 cup Cheddar cheese, green onions, onion powder, salt and garlic powder in medium bowl. Stir in bacon. Fill each pepper half with about 1 tablespoon cheese mixture. Sprinkle with remaining ½ cup Cheddar cheese, almond flour, if desired, and Parmesan cheese.

3 Preheat air fryer to 370°F. Line basket with parchment paper or foil; spray lightly with nonstick cooking spray.

4 Cook in batches 5 to 7 minutes or until cheese is melted and browned but peppers are still firm.

**Jalapeño peppers can sting and irritate the skin, so wear rubber gloves when handling peppers and do not touch your eyes.

CALORIES
110

TOTAL FAT
10g

CARBS
2g

NET CARBS
2g

DIETARY FIBER
0g

PROTEIN
4g

BUFFALO WINGS
MAKES 4 SERVINGS

CALORIES
320

TOTAL FAT
25g

CARBS
2g

NET CARBS
1g

DIETARY FIBER
1g

PROTEIN
20g

1 cup hot pepper sauce
⅓ cup olive oil, plus additional for brushing
½ teaspoon ground red pepper
½ teaspoon garlic powder
½ teaspoon Worcestershire sauce

⅛ teaspoon black pepper
1 pound chicken wings, tips discarded, separated at joints
Keto-friendly blue cheese or ranch dressing
Celery sticks (optional)

1 Combine hot pepper sauce, ⅓ cup oil, red pepper, garlic powder, Worcestershire sauce and black pepper in small saucepan; cook over medium heat 20 minutes. Remove from heat; pour sauce into large bowl.

2 Preheat air fryer to 370°F. Brush wings with additional oil. Cook in batches 16 to 18 minutes or until golden brown and cooked through, shaking halfway through cooking.

3 Transfer wings to bowl of sauce; stir to coat. Serve with blue cheese dressing and celery sticks, if desired.

BACON-WRAPPED TERIYAKI SHRIMP

MAKES 6 SERVINGS

CALORIES
260

TOTAL FAT
19g

CARBS
3g

NET CARBS
3g

DIETARY FIBER
0g

PROTEIN
17g

1 pound large raw shrimp, peeled and deveined (with tails on)

¼ cup sugar-free teriyaki marinade

12 slices bacon, cut in half crosswise

1 Place shrimp in large resealable food storage bag. Add teriyaki marinade; seal bag and turn to coat. Marinate in refrigerator 15 to 20 minutes.

2 Remove shrimp from bag; reserve marinade. Wrap each shrimp with 1 piece bacon. Brush bacon with some of reserved marinade.

3 Preheat air fryer to 390°F. Line basket with parchment paper or foil; spray lightly with nonstick cooking spray.

4 Cook 4 to 6 minutes or until bacon is crisp and shrimp are pink and opaque.

TIP

Do not use thick-cut bacon for this recipe, because the bacon will not be completely cooked when the shrimp are cooked through.

ASPARAGUS FRITTATA PROSCIUTTO CUPS
MAKES 12 CUPS (6 SERVINGS)

CALORIES
270

TOTAL
FAT
18g

CARBS
5g

NET
CARBS
4g

DIETARY
FIBER
1g

PROTEIN
22g

1 tablespoon olive oil
1 small red onion, finely chopped
1½ cups sliced asparagus (½-inch pieces)
1 clove garlic, minced
12 thin slices prosciutto

8 eggs
½ cup (2 ounces) grated white Cheddar cheese
¼ cup grated Parmesan cheese
2 tablespoons whipping cream
⅛ teaspoon black pepper

1 Heat oil in large skillet over medium heat. Add onion; cook and stir 4 minutes or until softened. Add asparagus and garlic; cook and stir 8 minutes or until asparagus is crisp-tender. Set aside to cool slightly.

2 Preheat air fryer to 370°F. Lightly spray 12 standard (2½-inch) silicone muffin cups with nonstick cooking spray.

3 Line each prepared muffin cup with prosciutto slice. (Prosciutto should cover cup as much as possible, with edges extending above muffin pan.) Whisk eggs, Cheddar, Parmesan, cream and pepper in large bowl until well blended. Stir in asparagus mixture until blended. Pour into prosciutto-lined cups, filling about three-fourths full.

4 Cook in batches 12 to 15 minutes or until frittatas are puffed and golden brown and edges are pulling away from cups. Cool in cups 5 minutes. Remove to wire racks; serve warm or at room temperature.

KALE CHIPS
MAKES 6 SERVINGS

1 large bunch kale (about 1 pound)
1 tablespoon olive oil
1 teaspoon garlic powder
½ teaspoon salt
½ teaspoon black pepper

1 Wash kale and pat dry with paper towels. Remove center ribs and stems; discard. Cut leaves into 2- to 3-inch-wide pieces.

2 Combine leaves, oil, garlic powder, salt and pepper in large bowl; toss to coat.

3 Preheat air fryer to 390°F.

4 Cook in batches 3 to 4 minutes or until edges are lightly browned and leaves are crisp. Cool completely. Store in airtight container.

CALORIES
60

TOTAL FAT
3g

CARBS
7g

NET CARBS
4g

DIETARY FIBER
3g

PROTEIN
3g

HOT TUNA SNACKS

MAKES 6 SERVINGS

CALORIES
83

TOTAL FAT
5g

CARBS
2g

NET CARBS
1g

DIETARY FIBER
1g

PROTEIN
9g

1 can (6 ounces) water-packed chunk light tuna, well drained
4 ounces cream cheese
1 tablespoon chopped fresh parsley
1 tablespoon minced onion

½ teaspoon dried oregano
½ teaspoon black pepper
18 (½-inch-thick) slices seedless cucumber
18 capers (optional)

1 Preheat air fryer to 350°F. Line basket with parchment paper or foil; spray lightly with nonstick cooking spray.

2 Combine tuna, cream cheese, parsley, onion, oregano and pepper in medium bowl; mix well. Mound about 1 tablespoon tuna mixture on top of each cucumber slice. If desired cold; place on serving plate and garnish with capers.

3 Cook 5 to 7 minutes or until tops are puffed and brown. Transfer to serving plate and garnish with capers.

NOTE

Capers are the flower buds of a bush native to the Mediterranean and parts of India. The buds are picked, sun-dried, then pickled. Capers should be rinsed before using to remove excess salt.

ZUCCHINI PIZZA BITES

MAKES 6 SERVINGS

CALORIES
113

TOTAL
FAT
8g

CARBS
3g

NET
CARBS
2g

DIETARY
FIBER
1g

PROTEIN
7g

⅓ cup salsa

¼ pound chorizo sausage*

2 small zucchini, trimmed and cut diagonally into ¼-inch-thick slices

6 tablespoons shredded mozzarella cheese

Chorizo, a spicy pork sausage, is common in both Mexican and Spanish cooking. The Mexican variety (which is the kind most widely available in the U.S.) is made from raw pork while the Spanish variety is traditionally made from smoked pork. If chorizo is unavailable, substitute any variety of spicy sausage.

1 Place salsa in fine-mesh strainer and press out excess moisture; set aside to drain. Remove sausage from casing. Heat small skillet over medium heat. Add sausage; cook and stir 5 minutes or until cooked through; drain fat.

2 Preheat air fryer to 350°F. Line basket with parchment paper or foil; spray lightly with nonstick cooking spray.

3 Spoon 1 teaspoon drained salsa on each zucchini slice; top with chorizo and sprinkle with cheese.

4 Cook 5 to 7 minutes or until cheese is melted.

CRAB STUFFED MUSHROOMS
MAKES 12 SERVINGS

CALORIES
80

TOTAL
FAT
6g

CARBS
2g

NET
CARBS
2g

DIETARY
FIBER
0g

PROTEIN
6g

2 cans (6 ounces each) lump crabmeat, drained

½ cup (2 ounces) shredded Monterey Jack cheese

⅓ cup finely chopped green onions

3 tablespoons mayonnaise

2 tablespoons shredded Parmesan cheese

1 tablespoon Worcestershire sauce

1 teaspoon minced garlic

1 pound white mushrooms (about 24 mushrooms), stems removed

2 tablespoons almond flour

1 Preheat air fryer to 390°F. Line basket with parchment paper; spray lightly with nonstick cooking spray.

2 Combine crabmeat, Monterey Jack, green onions, mayonnaise, Parmesan, Worcestershire sauce and garlic in medium bowl; gently mix. Spoon evenly into mushroom caps, flattening slightly, if necessary. Top evenly with almond flour.

3 Cook in batches 5 to 7 minutes or until heated through.

POBLANO PEPPER KABOBS

MAKES 4 SERVINGS

CALORIES
145

TOTAL
FAT
9g

CARBS
3g

NET
CARBS
2g

DIETARY
FIBER
1g

PROTEIN
13g

1 large poblano pepper*

4 ounces smoked turkey breast, cut into 8 cubes

4 ounces pepper jack cheese, cut into 8 cubes

¼ cup salsa (optional)

Poblano peppers can sting and irritate the skin, so wear rubber gloves when handling peppers and do not touch your eyes.

1 Fill medium saucepan half full with water; bring to a boil over medium-high heat. Add poblano; cook 1 minute. Drain. Core, seed and cut pepper into 8 bite-size pieces.

2 Preheat air fryer to 350°F. Line basket with parchment paper or foil; spray lightly with nonstick cooking spray. Thread 1 piece pepper, 1 piece turkey and 1 piece cheese onto each skewer. Repeat, ending with cheese and breaking skewers if necessary to fit basket.

3 Cook 5 to 7 minutes or until cheese is just starting to melt. Serve with salsa, if desired.

CRISPY CHEESE CHIPS
MAKES 8 SERVINGS

CALORIES
88

TOTAL
FAT
6g

CARBS
2g

NET
CARBS
2g

DIETARY
FIBER
0g

PROTEIN
7g

1½ cups (6 ounces) shredded mozzarella cheese*
½ cup grated Parmesan cheese
1 teaspoon chili powder
1 teaspoon black pepper

4 green onions (optional)

Shred cheese using largest holes on box grater. If purchasing shredded cheese, look for "chef-style" cheese which is grated into larger than usual pieces.

1 Preheat air fryer to 350°F. Line air fryer basket with parchment paper.

2 Place mozzarella in colander with large holes; shake to separate large shreds of cheese from smaller shreds. Save small shreds for another use. Remove large shreds to medium bowl; add Parmesan, chili powder and black pepper to medium bowl; toss to blend.

3 Sprinkle about ½ to 1 tablespoon cheese mixture in single layer in air fryer making lacy 2-inch circles. Cook 3 to 4 minutes or until cheese melts and turns golden brown. Remove to parchment-lined baking sheet; cool completely. Repeat with remaining cheese mixture. Store in airtight container until ready to serve.

4 If desired, cut single slit in each green onion by running tip of paring knife down the length of each green top once. Slice green tips crosswise into thin ribbons. Garnish cheese chips with ribbons.

NOTE

Cheese crisps are extremely hot and pliable when they are first removed from the air fryer, but become crispy and chewy as they cool. They are easily molded if draped over a rolling pin.

INDIVIDUAL SPINACH & BACON QUICHES
MAKES 12 SERVINGS

CALORIES
180

TOTAL FAT
12g

CARBS
4g

NET CARBS
3g

DIETARY FIBER
1g

PROTEIN
16g

3 slices bacon

½ small onion, diced

1 package (10 ounces) frozen chopped spinach, thawed and squeezed dry

½ teaspoon black pepper

⅛ teaspoon ground nutmeg

Pinch salt

3 eggs, lightly beaten

1 container (15 ounces) whole-milk ricotta cheese

2 cups (8 ounces) shredded mozzarella cheese

1 cup grated Parmesan cheese

1 Cook bacon in large skillet over medium-high heat until crisp. Drain on paper towels until cool enough to handle. Crumble bacon.

2 Heat same skillet with bacon drippings over medium heat. Add onion; cook and stir 5 minutes or until tender. Add spinach, pepper, nutmeg and salt; cook and stir 3 minutes or until liquid is evaporated. Remove from heat. Stir in bacon; set aside to cool.

3 Preheat air fryer to 370°F. Lightly spray 12 standard (2½-inch) silicone muffin cups with nonstick cooking spray.

4 Whisk eggs in large bowl. Add cheeses; stir until well blended. Add cooled spinach mixture; mix well. Spoon evenly into prepared muffin cups.

5 Cook in batches 12 to 15 minutes or until edges are firm to the touch. Cool in cups 5 minutes. Remove to wire racks; cool completely.

PROSCIUTTO-WRAPPED ASPARAGUS WITH GARLIC MAYONNAISE
MAKES 8 SERVINGS

CALORIES
210

TOTAL FAT
20g

CARBS
2g

NET CARBS
1g

DIETARY FIBER
1g

PROTEIN
5g

1 package (about 3 ounces) prosciutto, cut lengthwise into 16 strips

16 medium asparagus spears, trimmed

1 tablespoon olive oil

Black pepper (optional)

¾ cup mayonnaise

1 teaspoon lemon juice

1 clove garlic, minced

1 Preheat air fryer to 390°F. Line air fryer basket with foil or parchment paper.

2 Wrap 1 piece of prosciutto around each asparagus spear. Brush asparagus with oil; sprinkle with pepper, if desired.

3 Cook in batches 8 to 10 minutes, shaking occasionally during cooking, until tender.

4 Meanwhile for garlic mayonnaise, combine mayonnaise, lemon juice and garlic in small bowl until well blended. Serve asparagus warm with garlic mayonnaise.

CALORIES
160

TOTAL
FAT
14g

CARBS
3g

NET
CARBS
2g

DIETARY
FIBER
1g

PROTEIN
6g

TOASTED CHEESE KABOBS
MAKES 12 SERVINGS

8 thick slices Keto Bread
(recipe follows)

3 thick slices sharp Cheddar cheese

3 thick slices Monterey Jack or
Colby Jack cheese

2 tablespoons butter, melted

1 Cut each slice bread into 1-inch squares. Cut each slice cheese into 1-inch squares. Make small sandwiches with one square of bread and one square of each type of cheese. Top with second square of bread. Brush sandwiches with butter.

2 Preheat air fryer to 370°F. Cook sandwich squares 2 to 3 minutes or until golden brown and cheese is slightly melted.

3 Place sandwiches on the ends of short wooden skewers, if desired, or eat as finger food.

KETO BREAD
MAKES 1 LOAF (16 SLICES)

7 tablespoons butter, divided

2 cups almond flour

3½ teaspoons baking powder

½ teaspoon salt

6 eggs at room temperature,
separated*

¼ teaspoon cream of tartar

*Discard 1 egg yolk.

1 Preheat oven to 375°F. Generously grease 8X4-inch loaf pan with 1 tablespoon butter. Melt remaining 6 tablespoons butter; cool slightly.

2 Combine almond flour, baking powder and salt in medium bowl. Add melted butter and 5 egg yolks; stir until blended.

3 Place egg whites and cream of tartar in bowl of electric stand mixer; attach whip attachment to mixer. Whip egg whites on high speed 1 to 2 minutes or until stiff peaks form.

4 Stir one third of egg whites into almond flour mixture until well blended. Gently fold in remaining egg whites until thoroughly blended. Scrape batter into prepared pan; smooth top.

5 Bake 25 to 30 minutes or until top is light brown and dry and toothpick inserted into center comes out clean. Cool in pan on wire rack 10 minutes. Remove from pan; cool completely.

QUICK AND EASY STUFFED MUSHROOMS
MAKES 8 SERVINGS

CALORIES
50

TOTAL
FAT
4g

CARBS
4g

NET
CARBS
3g

DIETARY
FIBER
1g

PROTEIN
2g

16 large mushrooms
½ cup sliced celery
½ cup sliced onion
1 clove garlic
½ cup almond flour

1 teaspoon Worcestershire sauce
½ teaspoon dried marjoram
⅛ teaspoon ground red pepper
   Pinch paprika

1 Remove stems from mushrooms; reserve caps. Place mushroom stems, celery, onion and garlic in food processor; process using on/off pulses until vegetables are finely chopped.

2 Spray large skillet with nonstick cooking spray. Add vegetable mixture; cook and stir over medium heat 5 minutes or until onion is tender. Remove to bowl. Stir in almond flour, Worcestershire sauce, marjoram and red pepper.

3 Preheat air fryer to 390°F. Line basket with parchment paper; spray lightly with nonstick cooking spray.

4 Fill mushroom caps evenly with mixture, pressing down firmly. Spray tops with nonstick cooking spray. Sprinkle with paprika.

5 Cook in batches 5 to 7 minutes or until heated through.

NOTE

Mushrooms can be stuffed up to 1 day ahead. Refrigerate filled mushroom caps, covered, until ready to cook.

CHICKEN, TURKEY & DUCK

LEMON PEPPER CHICKEN

MAKES 4 SERVINGS

⅓ cup lemon juice

¼ cup finely chopped onion

2 tablespoons olive oil

1 tablespoon black pepper

3 cloves garlic, minced

2 teaspoons grated lemon peel

½ teaspoon salt

4 boneless skinless chicken breasts (about 1 pound)

1 Combine lemon juice, onion, oil, pepper, garlic, lemon peel and salt in small bowl; stir to blend. Pour marinade over chicken in large resealable food storage bag. Seal bag; knead to coat. Refrigerate at least 4 hours or overnight.

2 Preheat air fryer to 370°F. Line basket with parchment paper or foil; spray lightly with nonstick cooking spray.

3 Remove chicken from marinade; discard marinade. Cook in batches 15 to 20 minutes or until chicken is browned and no longer pink in center.

CALORIES
210

TOTAL FAT
10g

CARBS
4g

NET CARBS
3g

DIETARY FIBER
1g

PROTEIN
26g

CILANTRO-STUFFED CHICKEN BREASTS

MAKES 4 SERVINGS

CALORIES
180

TOTAL
FAT
9g

CARBS
1g

NET
CARBS
1g

DIETARY
FIBER
0g

PROTEIN
21g

2 cloves garlic
1 cup packed fresh cilantro leaves
1 tablespoon plus 2 teaspoons soy sauce, divided

1 tablespoon olive oil
4 boneless chicken breasts (about 1¼ pounds)
1 tablespoon dark sesame oil

1 Mince garlic in blender or food processor. Add cilantro; process until cilantro is minced. Add 2 teaspoons soy sauce and olive oil; process until paste forms.

2 With rubber spatula or fingers, distribute about 1 tablespoon cilantro mixture evenly under skin of each chicken breast, taking care not to puncture skin.

3 Preheat air fryer to 390°F. Line basket with parchment paper or foil; spray lightly with nonstick cooking spray.

4 Combine remaining 1 tablespoon soy sauce and sesame oil in small bowl; stir to blend. Brush soy sauce mixture evenly over chicken.

5 Cook in batches 15 to 20 minutes or until chicken is no longer pink in center.

LEMONY GREEK CHICKEN
MAKES 4 TO 6 SERVINGS

CALORIES
240

TOTAL
FAT
12g

CARBS
0g

NET
CARBS
0g

DIETARY
FIBER
0g

PROTEIN
32g

1 cut-up whole chicken
   (about 3 to 4 pounds)
1 tablespoon olive oil
2 teaspoons Greek seasoning

1 teaspoon salt
1 teaspoon black pepper
  Lemon slices (optional)

1 Preheat air fryer to 390°F. Spray basket with nonstick cooking spray.

2 Brush chicken with oil. Combine Greek seasoning, salt and pepper in small bowl; sprinkle over both sides of chicken.

3 Cook 20 to 25 minutes or until brown and crisp on all sides and cooked through (165°F). Serve warm. Garnish with lemon.

DUCK BREASTS WITH BALSAMIC SAUCE
MAKES 4 SERVINGS

CALORIES
390

TOTAL
FAT
22g

CARBS
5g

NET
CARBS
5g

DIETARY
FIBER
0g

PROTEIN
42g

4 boneless duck breasts (6 ounces each)
  Salt and black pepper
3 tablespoons balsamic vinegar

2 tablespoons lemon juice
1 tablespoon olive oil
1 shallot, minced

1 Score skin on duck breasts with tip of sharp knife in crosshatch pattern, being careful to cut only into the fat and not the meat. Season both sides of duck with salt and pepper.

2 Preheat air fryer to 370°F. Cook in batches 22 to 24 minutes or until medium rare (130°F). Remove duck to plate; let stand 10 minutes before slicing.

3 Combine vinegar and lemon juice in small bowl; mix well. Heat oil in small skillet. Add shallot; cook and stir over medium heat 2 to 3 minutes or until translucent. Add vinegar mixture; cook and stir about 5 minutes or until slightly thickened. Season with salt and pepper.

4 To serve, slice duck and drizzle with sauce.

PESTO TURKEY MEATBALLS
MAKES 4 SERVINGS

CALORIES
390

TOTAL
FAT
23g

CARBS
12g

NET
CARBS
8g

DIETARY
FIBER
4g

PROTEIN
37g

1 pound ground turkey
⅓ cup prepared pesto
⅓ cup grated Parmesan cheese, plus additional for garnish
¼ cup almond flour
1 egg
2 green onions, finely chopped
½ teaspoon salt, divided

3 tablespoons olive oil, divided
2 cloves garlic, minced
⅛ teaspoon red pepper flakes
1 can (28 ounces) whole tomatoes, undrained, crushed with hands or coarsely chopped
1 tablespoon tomato paste
Zucchini noodles (optional)

1 Combine turkey, pesto, ⅓ cup cheese, almond flour, egg, green onions and ¼ teaspoon salt in medium bowl; mix well. Shape mixture into 24 balls (about 1¼ inches). Refrigerate meatballs while preparing sauce.

2 Heat 2 tablespoons oil in large saucepan or Dutch oven over medium heat. Add garlic and red pepper flakes; cook and stir 2 minutes. Add tomatoes with liquid, tomato paste and remaining ¼ teaspoon salt; cook 15 minutes, stirring occasionally.

3 Preheat air fryer to 390°F. Line basket with parchment paper or foil; spray lightly with nonstick cooking spray.

4 Brush meatballs with remaining 1 tablespoon oil. Cook meatballs in batches 12 to 14 minutes or until cooked through, shaking halfway through cooking. Serve over zucchini noodles, if desired. Garnish with additional cheese.

EASY AIR-FRIED CHICKEN THIGHS

MAKES 4 SERVINGS

CALORIES
130

TOTAL
FAT
5g

CARBS
1g

NET
CARBS
1g

DIETARY
FIBER
0g

PROTEIN
20g

8 bone-in or boneless chicken thighs with skin (about 1½ pounds)
½ teaspoon garlic powder
½ teaspoon onion powder

½ teaspoon dried oregano
½ teaspoon ground thyme
½ teaspoon paprika
¼ teaspoon salt
½ teaspoon black pepper

1 Place chicken in large resealable food storage bag. Combine garlic powder, onion powder, oregano, thyme, paprika, salt and pepper in small bowl; mix well. Add to chicken; shake until spices are distributed.

2 Preheat air fryer to 350°F. Line basket with parchment paper or foil; spray lightly with nonstick cooking spray.

3 Cook in batches 20 to 25 minutes until golden browned and cooked through, turning chicken halfway through cooking.

BUTTERMILK AIR-FRIED CHICKEN
MAKES 6 SERVINGS

CALORIES
310

TOTAL
FAT
23g

CARBS
10g

NET
CARBS
6g

DIETARY
FIBER
4g

PROTEIN
20g

1 cut-up whole chicken
   (2½ to 3 pounds)
1 cup buttermilk
2 cups almond flour

½ teaspoon salt
½ teaspoon ground red pepper
¼ teaspoon garlic powder

1 Place chicken pieces in large resealable food storage bag. Pour buttermilk over chicken. Close and refrigerate; let marinate at least 2 hours.

2 Combine almond flour, salt, red pepper and garlic powder in large shallow bowl.

3 Preheat air fryer to 390°F. Spray basket with nonstick cooking spray.

4 Remove chicken pieces from buttermilk; coat with flour mixture. Spray chicken with nonstick cooking spray. Cook 20 to 25 minutes or until brown and crisp on all sides and cooked through (165°F). Serve warm.

TURKEY AND VEGGIE MEATBALLS WITH FENNEL
MAKES 6 SERVINGS

CALORIES
170

TOTAL
FAT
8g

CARBS
3g

NET
CARBS
2g

DIETARY
FIBER
1g

PROTEIN
23g

1 pound lean ground turkey	2 egg whites
½ cup finely chopped green onions	2 cloves garlic, minced
½ cup finely chopped green bell pepper	½ teaspoon Italian seasoning
⅓ cup almond flour	¼ teaspoon fennel seeds
2 tablespoons whipping cream	¼ teaspoon salt
¼ cup shredded carrot	⅛ teaspoon red pepper flakes (optional)
¼ cup grated Parmesan cheese	1 teaspoon olive oil

1 Combine all ingredients except oil in large bowl; mix well. Shape into 36 (1-inch) balls.

2 Preheat air fryer to 390°F. Line basket with parchment paper or foil; spray lightly with nonstick cooking spray.

3 Brush meatballs with oil. Cook meatballs in batches 12 to 14 minutes or until cooked through, shaking halfway through cooking.

SERVING SUGGESTION

Top with marinara sauce.

CHICKEN SALAD BOWL

MAKES 4 SERVINGS

CALORIES
570

TOTAL FAT
44g

CARBS
18g

NET CARBS
9g

DIETARY FIBER
9g

PROTEIN
30g

CHICKEN

- 1 tablespoon olive oil
- 1 teaspoon salt
- 1 teaspoon dried oregano
- 1 teaspoon paprika
- ½ teaspoon black pepper
- 1 clove garlic, minced
- 1 pound chicken tenders, cut in half

SALAD AND DRESSING

- ⅓ cup olive oil
- 3 tablespoons red wine vinegar
- 1 clove garlic, minced
  Salt and black pepper
- 1 cup grape tomatoes, halved
- 1 cucumber, halved crosswise and cut into sticks
- 1 red bell pepper, sliced
- 2 avocados, thinly sliced
- 2 radishes, thinly sliced
  Leaf lettuce and arugula
  Black and white sesame seeds

1 Combine 1 tablespoon oil, 1 teaspoon salt, oregano, paprika, ½ teaspoon black pepper and 1 clove garlic in large bowl. Add chicken; toss until well blended.

2 Preheat air fryer to 370°F. Line basket with parchment paper or foil; spray lightly with nonstick cooking spray.

3 Cook in batches 6 to 8 minutes or until chicken is no longer pink in center, turning halfway through cooking.

4 For dressing, whisk ⅓ cup oil, vinegar and 1 clove garlic in small bowl. Season to taste with salt and black pepper.

5 Place tomatoes, cucumber, bell pepper, avocados, radishes and lettuce in serving bowls; drizzle with dressing. Slice chicken and place on salads.

CHICKEN AND SAUSAGE SUPPER
MAKES 6 SERVINGS

⅓ cup olive oil

2 tablespoons balsamic vinegar

1 teaspoon salt

1 teaspoon garlic powder

½ teaspoon black pepper

¼ teaspoon red pepper flakes

3 pounds bone-in chicken thighs and drumsticks

1 pound uncooked sweet Italian sausage (4 to 5 links), cut diagonally into 2-inch pieces

6 small red onions (about 1 pound), each cut into 6 wedges

3½ cups broccoli florets

CALORIES
430

TOTAL FAT
25g

CARBS
12g

NET CARBS
10g

DIETARY FIBER
2g

PROTEIN
41g

1 Preheat air fryer to 390°F. Line basket with parchment paper or foil; spray lightly with nonstick cooking spray.

2 Whisk oil, vinegar, salt, garlic powder, black pepper and red pepper flakes in small bowl until well blended. Combine chicken, sausage and onions in large bowl. Drizzle with oil mixture; toss until well coated.

3 Spread mixture of chicken, sausage, onions and broccoli in single layer in air fryer. Cook in batches 20 to 25 minutes. (Chicken thighs should be skin side up). Remove each batch to large baking sheet.

BLUE CHEESE STUFFED CHICKEN BREASTS

MAKES 4 SERVINGS

½ cup crumbled blue cheese

2 tablespoons butter, softened, divided

¾ teaspoon dried thyme

Salt and black pepper

4 bone-in skin-on chicken breasts

1 tablespoon lemon juice

1 Combine cheese, 1 tablespoon butter and thyme in small bowl; stir to blend. Season with salt and pepper.

2 Loosen chicken skin by pushing fingers between skin and meat, taking care not to tear skin. Spread cheese mixture under skin; massage skin to spread mixture evenly over chicken breast.

3 Melt remaining 1 tablespoon butter in small bowl; stir in lemon juice until blended. Brush mixture over chicken. Sprinkle with salt and pepper.

4 Preheat air fryer to 370°F. Line basket with parchment paper or foil; spray lightly with nonstick cooking spray. Cook 15 to 20 minutes or until chicken is cooked through.

CALORIES
240

TOTAL FAT
13g

CARBS
1g

NET CARBS
1g

DIETARY FIBER
0g

PROTEIN
30g

SASSY CHICKEN & PEPPERS

MAKES 4 SERVINGS

1 tablespoon Mexican seasoning*

4 boneless skinless chicken breasts (about ¼ pound each)

1 red onion, sliced

1 medium red bell pepper, cut into thin strips

1 medium yellow or green bell pepper, cut into thin strips

½ cup chunky salsa or chipotle salsa

Lime wedges (optional)

If Mexican seasoning is not available, substitute 1 teaspoon chili powder, ½ teaspoon ground cumin, ½ teaspoon salt and ⅛ teaspoon ground red pepper.

1 Preheat air fryer to 390°F. Line basket with parchment paper or foil; spray lightly with nonstick cooking spray.

2 Sprinkle Mexican seasoning over both sides of chicken, onion and peppers.

3 Cook in batches 15 to 20 minutes or until chicken is no longer pink in center and vegetables are tender.

4 Serve chicken over vegetable mixture with salsa. Garnish with lime wedges.

CALORIES
224

TOTAL FAT
8g

CARBS
11g

NET CARBS
8g

DIETARY FIBER
3g

PROTEIN
27g

JALAPEÑO-LIME CHICKEN

MAKES 8 SERVINGS

1 tablespoon olive oil

1 tablespoon minced jalapeño pepper*

1 tablespoon lime juice

1 clove garlic, minced

1 teaspoon chili powder

½ teaspoon black pepper

⅛ teaspoon salt

8 bone-in chicken thighs

Jalapeño peppers can sting and irritate the skin, so wear rubber gloves when handling peppers and do not touch your eyes.

1 Preheat air fryer to 350°F. Line basket with parchment paper or foil; spray lightly with nonstick cooking spray. Line large baking sheet with parchment paper.

2 Combine oil, jalapeño, lime juice, garlic, chili powder, black pepper and salt in small bowl. Brush chicken with half of jalapeño mixture.

3 Cook in batches 10 to 15 minutes. Turn chicken; brush with jalapeño mixture. Cook 10 to 15 minutes or until golden browned and cooked through. Remove each batch to prepared baking sheet.

CALORIES
467

TOTAL FAT
32g

CARBS
11g

NET CARBS
10g

DIETARY FIBER
1g

PROTEIN
33g

SPICY LEMONY ALMOND CHICKEN

MAKES 4 SERVINGS

CALORIES
193

TOTAL
FAT
7g

CARBS
3g

NET
CARBS
2g

DIETARY
FIBER
1g

PROTEIN
28g

½ teaspoon paprika

½ teaspoon black pepper

¼ teaspoon salt

4 boneless skinless chicken breasts (about 1 pound), flattened to ¼-inch thickness

1 ounce slivered almonds, toasted*

¼ cup water

2 tablespoons lemon juice

2 tablespoons butter

2 teaspoons Worcestershire sauce

½ teaspoon grated lemon peel

To toast almonds, preheat air fryer to 350°F. Line with parchment paper or foil. Cook 3 to 4 minutes or until golden brown.

1 Preheat air fryer to 370°F. Line basket with parchment paper or foil; spray lightly with nonstick cooking spray.

2 Combine paprika, pepper and salt in small bowl; sprinkle evenly over both sides of chicken.

3 Cook in batches 15 to 20 minutes or until chicken is browned and no longer pink in center. Set aside on serving platter; sprinkle with almonds. Cover to keep warm.

4 Add water, lemon juice, butter and Worcestershire sauce to medium skillet. Cook and stir until pan sauces are reduced to ¼ cup, scraping bottom and side of skillet. Remove from heat, stir in lemon peel; spoon evenly over chicken.

TIP

To pound chicken, place between two pieces of plastic wrap. Starting in the center, pound chicken with a meat mallet to reach an even thickness.

RICOTTA AND SPINACH HASSELBACK CHICKEN
MAKES 2 SERVINGS

CALORIES
190

TOTAL
FAT
9g

CARBS
2g

NET
CARBS
2g

DIETARY
FIBER
0g

PROTEIN
26g

½ cup fresh baby spinach leaves
1 teaspoon olive oil
2 tablespoons ricotta cheese
2 boneless skinless chicken breasts
    (about 6 ounces each)

¼ teaspoon salt
⅛ teaspoon black pepper
2 tablespoons shredded Cheddar
    cheese

1 Place spinach and oil in small microwavable dish. Microwave on HIGH 20 to 30 seconds or until spinach is slightly wilted. Stir ricotta cheese into spinach; mix well.

2 Cut four diagonal slits three fourths of the way into each chicken breast (do not cut all the way through). Place about 1 teaspoon ricotta mixture into each slit. Sprinkle chicken with salt and pepper.

3 Preheat air fryer to 390°F. Line basket with parchment paper or foil; spray lightly with nonstick cooking spray.

4 Cook 12 minutes. Top chicken with Cheddar cheese. Cook 4 to 6 minutes or until cheese is melted, chicken is golden and juices run clear.

BEEF, PORK & LAMB

MEATBALLS AND RICOTTA
MAKES 10 SERVINGS (20 MEATBALLS)

CALORIES
450

TOTAL FAT
31g

CARBS
16g

NET CARBS
11g

DIETARY FIBER
5g

PROTEIN
26g

MEATBALLS

- ½ cup almond flour
- ½ cup milk
- 1 cup finely chopped yellow onion
- 2 green onions, finely chopped
- ½ cup grated Romano cheese, plus additional for serving
- 2 eggs, beaten
- ¼ cup finely chopped fresh parsley
- ¼ cup finely chopped fresh basil
- 2 cloves garlic, minced
- 2 teaspoons salt
- ¼ teaspoon black pepper
- 1 pound ground beef
- 1 pound ground pork
- 2 tablespoons olive oil

SAUCE

- 2 tablespoons olive oil
- 2 tablespoons butter
- 1 cup finely chopped yellow onion
- 1 clove garlic, minced
- 1 can (28 ounces) whole Italian plum tomatoes, coarsely chopped, juice reserved
- 1 can (28 ounces) crushed tomatoes
- 1 teaspoon salt
- ¼ teaspoon black pepper
- ¼ cup finely chopped fresh basil
- 1 to 1½ cups ricotta cheese

1 For meatballs, combine almond flour and milk in large bowl; mix well. Add 1 cup yellow onion, green onions, ½ cup Romano, eggs, parsley, ¼ cup basil, 2 cloves garlic, 2 teaspoons salt and ¼ teaspoon black pepper; mix well. Add beef and pork; mix gently but thoroughly until blended. Shape mixture by ¼ cupfuls into balls.

2 Preheat air fryer to 390°F. Line basket with parchment paper or foil; spray lightly with nonstick cooking spray.

3 Brush meatballs with 2 tablespoons oil. Cook meatballs in batches 12 to 14 minutes or until cooked through, shaking halfway through cooking.

4 For sauce, heat 2 tablespoons oil and butter in large saucepan over medium heat until butter is melted. Add 1 cup yellow onion; cook 8 minutes or until tender and lightly browned, stirring frequently. Add 1 clove garlic; cook and stir 1 minute or until fragrant. Add plum tomatoes with juice, crushed tomatoes, 1 teaspoon salt and ¼ teaspoon black pepper; bring to a simmer. Reduce heat to medium-low; cook 20 minutes, stirring occasionally.

5 Stir ¼ cup basil into sauce. Transfer meatballs and sauce to serving dish; dollop tablespoonfuls of ricotta between meatballs. Garnish with additional Romano.

BACON SMASHBURGER
MAKES 4 SERVINGS

4 slices bacon, cut in half
1 pound ground chuck
  Salt and black pepper

4 slices sharp Cheddar cheese
4 eggs (optional)
4 slices Romaine lettuce (optional)

1 Preheat air fryer to 400°F. Cook bacon 8 to 10 minutes. Remove from basket to paper towels; blot any grease from bacon. Set aside.

2 Preheat air fryer to 370°F. Line basket with parchment paper or foil; spray lightly with nonstick cooking spray. Divide beef into 4 portions and shape into patties. Season with salt and pepper.

3 Cook patties in batches 5 to 6 minutes; turn over. Top each patty with 1 slice cheese. Cook in batches 5 to 6 minutes or until cheese is melted and patties are cooked through. Remove to large plate; keep warm.

4 If desired, heat large skillet over medium heat. Crack eggs into skillet; cook over medium heat about 3 minutes or until whites are opaque and yolks are desired degree of doneness, flipping once, if desired, for overeasy. Place burgers on lettuce; top with eggs, if desired, and bacon.

PORK MEDALLIONS WITH MARSALA
MAKES 4 SERVINGS

1 pound pork tenderloin,
   cut into ½-inch slices
Salt and black pepper
2 tablespoons olive oil

1 clove garlic, minced
½ cup marsala wine
2 tablespoons chopped fresh
   parsley

1 Preheat air fryer to 370°F. Spray basket with nonstick cooking spray. Season pork with salt and pepper.

2 Cook 12 to 15 minutes or until cooked through.

3 Meanwhile, heat oil in medium skillet. Add garlic; cook and stir 1 minute. Add wine; cook 3 minutes. Stir in parsley. Simmer wine mixture 2 to 3 minutes or until slightly thickened. Serve over pork.

NOTE

Marsala is a rich, smoky-flavored wine imported from the Mediterranean island of Sicily. This sweet varietal is served with dessert or used for cooking. Dry Marsala is served as a before-dinner drink.

CALORIES
218

TOTAL FAT
10g

CARBS
1g

NET CARBS
0g

DIETARY FIBER
1g

PROTEIN
24g

BACON-TOMATO GRILLED CHEESE
MAKES 4 SERVINGS

CALORIES
530

TOTAL FAT
45g

CARBS
10g

NET CARBS
7g

DIETARY FIBER
3g

PROTEIN
27g

½ loaf Keto Bread, cut into 8 slices (page 56)

8 slices bacon, cut in half

4 slices sharp Cheddar cheese

4 slices Gouda cheese

4 tomato slices

1 Prepare Keto Bread.

2 Preheat air fryer to 400°F. Cook bacon 8 to 10 minutes. Remove from basket to paper towels; blot any grease from bacon.

3 Meanwhile, layer 1 slice of Cheddar, 1 slice of Gouda, 1 tomato slice and 2 slices bacon between 2 bread slices. Repeat with remaining ingredients.

4 Cook 3 to 5 minutes or until cheeses are melted and bread is golden brown.

MOROCCAN-STYLE LAMB CHOPS
MAKES 4 SERVINGS

CALORIES
173

TOTAL
FAT
8g

CARBS
1g

NET
CARBS
0g

DIETARY
FIBER
1g

PROTEIN
23g

1 tablespoon olive oil
1 teaspoon ground cumin
1 teaspoon ground coriander
¾ teaspoon salt
⅛ teaspoon ground cinnamon

⅛ teaspoon ground red pepper
4 center-cut lamb loin chops, cut 1 inch thick (about 1 pound)
2 cloves garlic, minced

1 Preheat air fryer to 370°F. Line basket with parchment paper or foil; spray lightly with nonstick cooking spray.

2 Combine oil, cumin, coriander, salt, cinnamon and red pepper in small bowl; mix well. Rub or brush oil mixture over both sides of lamb chops. Sprinkle garlic over both sides of lamb chops.

3 Cook in batches 12 to 14 minutes or until lamb chops are browned and no longer pink in middle, turning halfway through cooking. Remove to serving plate.

PORK WITH CUCUMBER PICO DE GALLO
MAKES 4 SERVINGS

½ of a medium unpeeled cucumber, seeded and finely chopped (4 ounces total)

2 medium tomatillos, papery skin removed, rinsed and chopped

2 tablespoons chopped cilantro leaves

⅛ teaspoon red pepper flakes

1 to 2 tablespoons lime juice

¼ teaspoon salt, divided

4 boneless center cut pork cutlets, trimmed of fat (about 1 pound)

¼ teaspoon coarsely ground black pepper

1 Combine cucumber, tomatillos, cilantro, red pepper flakes, lime juice, and ⅛ teaspoon salt in medium bowl; toss gently to blend.

2 Preheat air fryer to 370°F. Line basket with parchment paper or foil; spray lightly with nonstick cooking spray. Coat pork chops evenly with black pepper and remaining ⅛ teaspoon salt.

3 Cook 12 to 15 minutes or until cooked through. Serve with pico de gallo.

NOTE

To seed a cucumber easily, split cucumber in half lengthwise. Run the tip of a teaspoon down the center to remove seeds. This prevents the dish from being too watery and diluting the flavors.

CALORIES
231

TOTAL FAT
13g

CARBS
2g

NET CARBS
1g

DIETARY FIBER
1g

PROTEIN
23g

FLANK STEAK & ROASTED VEGETABLE SALAD
MAKES 4 SERVINGS

CALORIES
270

TOTAL
FAT
11g

CARBS
13g

NET
CARBS
7g

DIETARY
FIBER
6g

PROTEIN
29g

1 pound flank steak (1 inch thick), sliced across the grain into ½-inch strips

¾ teaspoon salt, divided

½ teaspoon black pepper, divided

2 tablespoons plus 1 teaspoon Dijon mustard, divided

1 tablespoon fresh lemon juice

1 tablespoon olive oil

1 tablespoon water

1½ pounds crisp-cooked asparagus spears, trimmed and cut into 2-inch lengths

Crisp-cooked baby carrots (optional)

6 cups mixed salad greens

1 Preheat air fryer to 370°F. Line basket with parchment paper or foil; spray lightly with nonstick cooking spray.

2 Sprinkle steak with ½ teaspoon salt and ¼ teaspoon pepper; rub with 2 tablespoons mustard. Cook in batches 8 to 10 minutes, turning halfway through cooking, until desired doneness.

3 Whisk lemon juice, oil, water, remaining 1 teaspoon mustard, ¼ teaspoon salt and ¼ teaspoon pepper in large bowl. Add asparagus, carrots, if desired, and greens to dressing in bowl; toss to coat. Divide salad and steak evenly onto serving plates.

PHILLY CHEESE STEAKS
MAKES 4 SERVINGS

CALORIES
310

TOTAL FAT
20g

CARBS
6g

NET CARBS
5g

DIETARY FIBER
1g

PROTEIN
27g

1 pound boneless beef rib-eye steaks, sliced ¼ inch thick

1 green bell pepper

1 medium onion, peeled and thinly sliced

2 tablespoons olive oil

½ teaspoon salt

½ teaspoon black pepper

¼ teaspoon red pepper flakes (optional)

4 slices American cheese

1 Preheat air fryer to 370°F. Line basket with parchment paper or foil; spray lightly with nonstick cooking spray.

2 Combine steaks, bell pepper, onion, oil, salt, black pepper and red pepper flakes, if desired, in large bowl; toss to coat.

3 Cook in batches 8 to 10 minutes, shaking and turning halfway through cooking, until desired doneness. Top with cheese; cook 1 minute or until cheese is melted.

PORK TENDERLOIN WITH AVOCADO-TOMATILLO SALSA
MAKES 4 SERVINGS

CALORIES
174

TOTAL FAT
6g

CARBS
4g

NET CARBS
2g

DIETARY FIBER
2g

PROTEIN
25g

2 medium tomatillos, husked* and diced

½ ripe medium avocado, diced

1 jalapeño pepper,** seeded and finely chopped

1 clove garlic, minced

2 tablespoons finely chopped red onion

1 tablespoon lime juice

1 to 2 tablespoons chopped fresh cilantro

⅛ teaspoon salt

1 teaspoon olive oil

1½ teaspoons chili powder

½ teaspoon ground cumin

1 pound pork tenderloin, cut into 1-inch slices

4 lime wedges (optional)

Remove the husk by pulling from the bottom to where it attaches at the stem, Wash before using.

**Jalapeño peppers can sting and irritate the skin, so wear rubber gloves when handling and do not touch your eyes.*

1 Combine tomatillos, avocado, jalapeño, garlic, onion, lime juice, cilantro and salt in small bowl; toss gently to blend. Set aside.

2 Preheat air fryer to 370°F. Line basket with parchment paper or foil; spray lightly with nonstick cooking spray.

3 Combine oil, chili powder and cumin in small bowl; stir to blend. Rub evenly on pork, pressing to allow spices to adhere.

4 Cook 12 to 15 minutes or until cooked through. Serve pork with salsa and lime wedges, if desired.

TIP

Choose firm tomatillos with dry husks that are not too ragged. Store in a paper bag in refrigerator for up to 1 month.

MINI MARINATED BEEF SKEWERS
MAKES 6 SERVINGS (3 SKEWERS EACH)

1 boneless beef top round steak (about 1 pound)	1 teaspoon dark sesame oil
2 tablespoons soy sauce	2 cloves garlic, minced
1 tablespoon dry sherry	18 cherry tomatoes (optional)
	Fresh greens (optional)

CALORIES
120

TOTAL FAT
4g

CARBS
2g

NET CARBS
1g

DIETARY FIBER
1g

PROTEIN
20g

1 Cut beef crosswise into 18 (⅛-inch-thick) slices. Place in large resealable food storage bag. Add soy sauce, sherry, oil and garlic. Seal bag; turn to coat. Marinate in refrigerator at least 30 minutes or up to 2 hours.

2 Meanwhile, soak 18 (6-inch) wooden skewers in water 2 minutes.

3 Preheat air fryer to 370°F. Spray basket with nonstick cooking spray. Drain beef; discard marinade. Weave beef accordion-style onto skewers, breaking skewers if necessary to fit basket.

4 Cook in batches 8 to 10 minutes or until desired doneness, turning halfway through cooking. Garnish with cherry tomatoes and greens. Serve warm.

ROSEMARY PORK WITH GARLIC AÏOLI
MAKES 8 SERVINGS

CALORIES
260

TOTAL FAT
18g

CARBS
1g

NET CARBS
1g

DIETARY FIBER
0g

PROTEIN
24g

PORK

2 pork tenderloins (about 1 pound each), cut into 1-inch slices
   Juice of 2 lemons
1 tablespoon olive oil
½ teaspoon dried rosemary
   Paprika to taste
   Salt and pepper to taste

AÏOLI

½ cup mayonnaise
2 tablespoons olive oil
2 tablespoons Dijon mustard
1 clove garlic, minced
⅛ teaspoon salt

1 Place pork, lemon juice, oil, rosemary, paprika, salt and pepper in shallow dish. Let stand 15 minutes to marinate.

2 Meanwhile, combine aïoli ingredients in small bowl; cover with plastic wrap and refrigerate until ready to serve. This may be prepared 48 hours in advance.

3 Preheat air fryer to 370°F. Line basket with parchment paper or foil; spray lightly with nonstick cooking spray.

4 Remove pork from marinade. Discard marinade. Cook 12 to 15 minutes or until cooked through. Arrange pork on serving platter. Serve warm with aïoli.

HERB-RUBBED PORK TENDERLOIN WITH MUSTARD SAUCE
MAKES 6 SERVINGS

CALORIES
210

TOTAL
FAT
10g

CARBS
1g

NET
CARBS
1g

DIETARY
FIBER
0g

PROTEIN
25g

1½ teaspoons Italian seasoning
¼ teaspoon black pepper
1 pork tenderloin (about 1½ pounds), trimmed of fat and cut into ½-inch slices
1½ teaspoons olive oil
1 shallot, minced

1 clove garlic, minced
½ cup chicken broth
⅓ cup whole milk
1 tablespoon Dijon mustard
¼ teaspoon salt

1 Preheat air fryer to 370°F. Spray basket with nonstick cooking spray. Combine Italian seasoning and pepper in small bowl. Rub evenly over pork.

2 Cook in batches 12 to 15 minutes or until cooked through.

3 Meanwhile, heat oil in medium skillet over medium heat. Add shallot and garlic; cook and stir 1 minute. Stir in broth, milk, mustard and salt; simmer 2 minutes. Serve pork with mustard sauce.

CHINESE PEPPERCORN BEEF

MAKES 4 SERVINGS

CALORIES
330

TOTAL
FAT
14g

CARBS
4g

NET
CARBS
3g

DIETARY
FIBER
1g

PROTEIN
43g

- 2 teaspoons whole black and pink peppercorns*
- 2 teaspoons coriander seeds
- 1 tablespoon olive oil
- 1 boneless beef top sirloin steak, about 1¼ inches thick (1¼ pounds), cut crosswise into thin slices
- 2 teaspoons dark sesame oil
- ½ cup thinly sliced shallots or sweet onion
- ½ cup beef broth
- 2 tablespoons soy sauce
- 1 tablespoon dry sherry
- 2 tablespoons thinly sliced green onion or chopped fresh cilantro

You may use all black peppercorns if preferred.

1 Preheat air fryer to 370°F. Line basket with parchment paper or foil; spray lightly with nonstick cooking spray. Place peppercorns and coriander seeds in small resealable food storage bag; seal bag. Coarsely crush spices using meat mallet or bottom of heavy saucepan. Brush olive oil over both sides of steak; sprinkle with peppercorn mixture, pressing lightly.

2 Cook in batches 8 to 10 minutes, turning halfway through cooking, until desired doneness.

3 Meanwhile, add sesame oil to large skillet; heat over medium heat. Add shallots; cook and stir 3 minutes. Add broth, soy sauce and sherry; simmer about 5 minutes. To serve, spoon sauce over steak; sprinkle with green onion.

PORK TENDERLOIN WITH SHERRY-MUSHROOM SAUCE
MAKES 4 SERVINGS

CALORIES
179

TOTAL
FAT
6g

CARBS
4g

NET
CARBS
3g

DIETARY
FIBER
1g

PROTEIN
26g

1 to 2 pork tenderloins (1 to 1½ pounds), cut into ½-inch slices
Salt and black pepper
1 tablespoon butter
1½ cups chopped button mushrooms or shiitake mushroom caps
2 tablespoons sliced green onion

1 clove garlic, minced
⅓ cup beef broth
1 tablespoon chopped fresh parsley
1 tablespoon dry sherry
½ teaspoon dried thyme

1 Preheat air fryer to 370°F. Spray basket with nonstick cooking spray. Season pork with salt and pepper.

2 Cook 12 to 15 minutes or until cooked through.

3 Meanwhile, melt butter in medium skillet over medium heat. Add mushrooms, green onion and garlic; cook and stir 3 to 5 minutes or until vegetables are tender. Stir in broth, parsley, sherry and thyme; bring to a boil. Cook and stir 2 minutes. Slice pork; serve with sauce.

PORK AND RED CABBAGE SLAW

MAKES 4 SERVINGS

CALORIES
222

TOTAL
FAT
7g

CARBS
11g

NET
CARBS
10g

DIETARY
FIBER
1g

PROTEIN
28g

1 pork tenderloin (about 1 pound), trimmed of fat and cut into ½-inch slices

1 cup plain yogurt

1 clove garlic, minced

1 teaspoon dried oregano

Grated peel of 1 lemon

2 cups shredded red cabbage

½ cup chopped green onions (green parts only)

2 tablespoons balsamic vinegar

1 tablespoon olive oil

½ teaspoon salt, divided

½ teaspoon black pepper, divided

1 Combine pork, yogurt, garlic, oregano and lemon peel in large resealable food storage bag; turn to coat. Cover; refrigerate 4 to 6 hours.

2 Combine cabbage, green onions, vinegar, oil, ¼ teaspoon salt and ¼ teaspoon pepper in medium bowl; refrigerate until ready to serve.

3 Preheat air fryer to 370°F. Line basket with parchment paper or foil; spray lightly with nonstick cooking spray.

4 Cook in batches 12 to 15 minutes or until cooked through. Serve with slaw.

FISH & SEAFOOD

SALMON WITH BOK CHOY
MAKES 4 SERVINGS

CALORIES
280

TOTAL FAT
15g

CARBS
8g

NET CARBS
7g

DIETARY FIBER
1g

PROTEIN
25g

3 tablespoons finely chopped fresh ginger

3 tablespoons unseasoned rice vinegar

2 cloves garlic, minced

1 tablespoon soy sauce

4 skinless salmon fillets (4 ounces each)

½ cup vegetable broth

1 teaspoon hoisin sauce

6 cups chopped bok choy

¼ cup sliced green onions

1 Preheat air fryer to 350°F. Line basket with parchment paper; spray lightly with nonstick cooking spray.

2 Combine ginger, vinegar, garlic and soy sauce in small bowl; stir to blend. Brush salmon with ginger mixture.

3 Cook in batches 8 to 10 minutes or until salmon easily flakes when tested with a fork.

4 Meanwhile, heat broth and hoisin sauce in large saucepan. Add bok choy; cook 10 to 12 minutes or until crisp-tender.

5 Top salmon with green onions; serve with bok choy.

FISH WITH THAI PESTO

MAKES 6 SERVINGS

CALORIES
530

TOTAL FAT
43g

CARBS
4g

NET CARBS
2g

DIETARY FIBER
2g

PROTEIN
33g

1 to 2 jalapeño peppers,* coarsely chopped

1 lemon

4 green onions, thinly sliced

2 tablespoons chopped fresh ginger

3 cloves garlic, minced

1½ cups lightly packed fresh basil leaves

1 cup lightly packed fresh cilantro leaves

¼ cup lightly packed fresh mint leaves

¼ cup unsalted roasted peanuts

2 tablespoons unsweetened shredded coconut

½ cup olive oil

2 pounds boneless fish fillets (such as salmon, halibut, cod or orange roughy)

Lemon and cucumber slices (optional)

Jalapeño peppers can sting and irritate the skin, so wear rubber gloves when handling peppers and do not touch your eyes.

1 Place jalapeños in blender or food processor.

2 Grate peel of lemon. Juice lemon to measure 2 tablespoons. Add peel and juice to blender.

3 Add green onions, ginger, garlic, basil, cilantro, mint, peanuts and coconut to blender; blend until finely chopped. With motor running, slowly pour in oil; blend until mixed. Spread solid thin layer of pesto over each fillet.

4 Preheat air fryer to 350°F. Line basket with parchment paper or foil; spray lightly with nonstick cooking spray.

5 Cook in batches 8 to 10 minutes or until fish is lightly crisped and easily flakes when tested with a fork. Garnish with lemon and cucumber slices.

KETO TUNA MELT

MAKES 4 SERVINGS

CALORIES
980

TOTAL FAT
80g

CARBS
9g

NET CARBS
6g

DIETARY FIBER
3g

PROTEIN
62g

½ loaf Keto Bread, cut into 8 slices (page 56)

¾ cup mayonnaise

2 teaspoons lemon juice

1 teaspoon salt

⅛ teaspoon black pepper

1 can (12 ounces) solid white albacore tuna, drained

1 can (12 ounces) chunk light tuna, drained

1 stalk celery, finely chopped (about ½ cup)

¼ cup minced red onion

8 slices Cheddar cheese

2 tablespoons butter

Optional toppings: tomato slices, onion rings, avocado slices, pickles and/or lettuce leaves

1 Prepare Keto Bread.

2 Preheat air fryer to 370°F. Combine mayonnaise, lemon juice, salt and pepper in large bowl. Add tuna, celery and onion; mix well. Spread butter evenly over bread slices; top evenly with tuna.

3 Cook in batches 3 to 4 minutes or until heated through and lightly browned. Top with cheese. Cook 1 to 2 minutes or until cheese is melted. Garnish with desired toppings.

FARM-RAISED CATFISH WITH BACON AND HORSERADISH
MAKES 6 SERVINGS

CALORIES
380

TOTAL FAT
30g

CARBS
4g

NET CARBS
4g

DIETARY FIBER
0g

PROTEIN
22g

2 tablespoons butter
¼ cup chopped onion
1 package (8 ounces) cream cheese, softened
¼ cup dry white wine or vegetable broth
2 tablespoons prepared horseradish

1 tablespoon Dijon mustard
½ teaspoon salt
⅛ teaspoon black pepper
6 farm-raised catfish fillets (4 to 5 ounces each)
4 slices bacon, crisp-cooked and crumbled

1 Preheat air fryer to 390°F. Line basket with parchment paper or foil; spray lightly with nonstick cooking spray.

2 Melt butter in small skillet over medium-high heat. Add onion; cook and stir until softened. Combine cream cheese, wine, horseradish, mustard, salt and pepper in small bowl; stir in onion. Brush over fish and top with crumbled bacon.

3 Cook in batches 8 to 10 minutes or until fish begins to flake when tested with a fork.

SEA BASS WITH AROMATIC VEGETABLES

MAKES 6 SERVINGS

CALORIES
250

TOTAL FAT
7g

CARBS
15g

NET CARBS
11g

DIETARY FIBER
4g

PROTEIN
31g

6 sea bass fillets or other firm-fleshed white fish (2 to 3 pounds)
   Salt and black pepper
2 tablespoons butter

2 bulbs fennel, thinly sliced
3 large carrots, julienned
3 large leeks, cleaned and thinly sliced

1 Preheat air fryer to 390°F. Line basket with parchment paper or foil; spray lightly with nonstick cooking spray. Season bass with salt and pepper.

2 Cook in batches 8 to 10 minutes or until fish begins to flake when tested with a fork.

3 Meanwhile, melt butter in large skillet over medium-high heat. Add fennel, carrots and leeks; cook and stir 6 to 8 minutes or until beginning to soften and lightly brown. Season with salt and pepper.

4 To serve, top each fillet with vegetables.

SALMON BURGERS WITH TARRAGON AÏOLI SAUCE
MAKES 4 SERVINGS

CALORIES
190

TOTAL FAT
14g

CARBS
6g

NET CARBS
4g

DIETARY FIBER
2g

PROTEIN
11g

TARRAGON AÏOLI SAUCE

- ⅓ cup sour cream
- 1½ tablespoons mayonnaise
- 1 tablespoon milk
- ½ teaspoon dried tarragon
- ¼ teaspoon salt
- ⅛ teaspoon black pepper

BURGER

- 1 can (6 ounces) pink salmon, drained
- ¼ cup almond flour
- ⅓ cup chopped green onions
- ¼ cup chopped fresh cilantro
- 2 egg whites
- 2 tablespoons lime juice
- ¼ teaspoon salt
- ⅛ teaspoon ground red pepper

1 For sauce, combine sour cream, mayonnaise, milk, tarragon, ¼ teaspoon salt and black pepper in medium bowl; stir to blend. Refrigerate until ready to use.

2 For burgers, combine salmon, almond flour, green onions, cilantro, egg whites, lime juice, ¼ teaspoon salt and red pepper in large bowl; mix well.

3 Preheat air fryer to 370°F. Line basket with parchment paper or foil; spray lightly with nonstick cooking spray.

4 Cook in batches 8 to 10 minutes, turning halfway through cooking. Serve with sauce.

TILAPIA WITH SPINACH AND FETA
MAKES 2 SERVINGS

CALORIES
230

TOTAL
FAT
10g

CARBS
6g

NET
CARBS
3g

DIETARY
FIBER
3g

PROTEIN
30g

1 teaspoon olive oil
1 clove garlic, minced
4 cups baby spinach
2 skinless tilapia fillets or other mild
   white fish (4 ounces each)

¼ teaspoon black pepper
2 ounces feta cheese, cut into
   2 (3-inch) pieces

1 Preheat air fryer to 390°F. Line basket with parchment paper or foil; spray lightly with nonstick cooking spray.

2 Heat oil in medium skillet over medium-low heat. Add garlic; cook and stir 30 seconds. Add spinach; cook just until wilted, stirring occasionally.

3 Season tilapia with pepper. Place one piece of cheese on each fillet; top with spinach mixture. Fold one end of each fillet up and over filling; secure with toothpick. Repeat with opposite end of each fillet.

4 Cook in batches 8 to 10 minutes or until fish begins to flake when tested with a fork.

SHRIMP WITH TOMATOES

MAKES 4 SERVINGS

CALORIES
112

TOTAL FAT
5g

CARBS
5g

NET CARBS
4g

DIETARY FIBER
1g

PROTEIN
13g

1½ teaspoons paprika
1 teaspoon Italian seasoning
½ teaspoon garlic powder
¼ teaspoon black pepper
½ pound (about 24) small raw shrimp, peeled (with tails on)

1 tablespoon olive oil
1½ cups halved grape tomatoes
½ cup sliced onion, separated into rings
Lime wedges (optional)

1 Preheat air fryer to 350°F. Line basket with parchment paper or foil; spray lightly with nonstick cooking spray. Combine paprika, Italian seasoning, garlic powder and pepper in small bowl; add to large resealable food storage bag. Add shrimp, seal bag and shake to coat.

2 Cook in batches 8 to 10 minutes, turning once halfway through cooking, until shrimp are pink and opaque. Toss tomatoes and onion into last batch of shrimp; cook 2 minutes or until vegetables are heated through. Serve with lime wedges, if desired.

SOUTHWESTERN TUNA SALAD
MAKES 4 SERVINGS (1 CUP PER SERVING)

CALORIES
180

TOTAL FAT
7g

CARBS
8g

NET CARBS
5g

DIETARY FIBER
3g

PROTEIN
21g

2 limes, juiced, divided

12 ounces raw tuna steaks (about 1 inch thick)

1 pint cherry or grape tomatoes, halved

¼ cup diced ripe avocado (¼ of medium avocado)

1 jalapeño pepper,* seeded and minced

1 green onion, chopped (green parts only)

1 tablespoon chopped fresh cilantro

1½ teaspoons canola oil

¼ teaspoon salt

¼ teaspoon ground cumin

⅛ teaspoon black pepper

Lime wedges (optional)

Jalapeño peppers can sting and irritate the skin, so wear rubber gloves when handling peppers and do not touch your eyes.

1 Place juice of one lime in glass baking dish or shallow bowl. Add tuna steaks. Marinate at room temperature 30 minutes, turning once.

2 Preheat air fryer to 370°F. Line basket with parchment paper or foil; spray lightly with nonstick cooking spray.

3 Cook in batches 12 to 15 minutes or until cooked through. Remove and set aside until cooled to room temperature. Cut into 1-inch pieces.

4 Combine tomatoes, avocado, jalapeño, green onion and cilantro in large bowl. Add tuna.

5 Whisk oil, remaining lime juice, salt, cumin and black pepper in small bowl. Pour over salad; toss to coat. Garnish with lime wedges.

HUNAN FISH FILLETS

MAKES 4 SERVINGS

CALORIES	
210	

CALORIES
210

TOTAL
FAT
10g

CARBS
1g

NET
CARBS
0g

DIETARY
FIBER
1g

PROTEIN
27g

3 tablespoons soy sauce

1 tablespoon finely chopped green onion

2 teaspoons dark sesame oil

1 clove garlic, minced

1 teaspoon minced fresh ginger

¼ teaspoon red pepper flakes

1 pound red snapper, scrod or cod fillets

1 Preheat air fryer to 390°F. Line basket with parchment paper or foil; spray lightly with nonstick cooking spray.

2 Combine soy sauce, green onion, oil, garlic, ginger and red pepper flakes in small bowl; stir to blend. Brush fish with soy sauce mixture.

3 Cook in batches 8 to 10 minutes or until fish begins to flake when tested with a fork.

DILLED SALMON IN PARCHMENT

MAKES 2 SERVINGS

2 skinless salmon fillets (4 ounces each)
1 tablespoon butter, melted
1 tablespoon lemon juice

1 tablespoon chopped fresh dill
1 tablespoon chopped shallots
¼ teaspoon salt
⅛ teaspoon black pepper

CALORIES
290

TOTAL FAT
21g

CARBS
1g

NET CARBS
1g

DIETARY FIBER
0g

PROTEIN
23g

1 Preheat air fryer to 370°F. Cut two pieces of parchment paper into 12-inch squares. Place fish fillets on parchment.

2 Combine butter and lemon juice in small bowl; drizzle over fish. Sprinkle with dill, shallots, salt and pepper. Wrap parchment around fish.

3 Cook 6 to 8 minutes or until fish is cooked through and easily flakes when tested with a fork.

FISH WITH LEMON-TARRAGON BUTTER
MAKES 2 SERVINGS

CALORIES
120

TOTAL FAT
5g

CARBS
1g

NET CARBS
1g

DIETARY FIBER
0g

PROTEIN
18g

2 teaspoons butter
4 teaspoons lemon juice, divided
½ teaspoon grated lemon peel
¼ teaspoon prepared mustard
¼ teaspoon dried tarragon

⅛ teaspoon salt
2 lean white fish fillets (4 ounces each),* rinsed and patted dry
¼ teaspoon paprika

Cod, orange roughy, flounder, haddock, halibut and sole can be used.

1 Combine butter, 2 teaspoons lemon juice, lemon peel, mustard, tarragon and salt in small bowl; mix well with fork.

2 Preheat air fryer to 390°F. Line basket with parchment paper or foil; spray lightly with nonstick cooking spray. Drizzle fish with remaining 2 teaspoons lemon juice; sprinkle one side of each fillet with paprika.

3 Cook fish, paprika side down; 8 to 10 minutes until fish is opaque in center and begins to flake when tested with a fork. Top with butter mixture.

SOY-MARINATED SALMON
MAKES 4 SERVINGS

¼ cup lime juice
¼ cup soy sauce
1 tablespoon grated fresh ginger
1 tablespoon minced garlic

¼ teaspoon black pepper
4 salmon fillets (7 to 8 ounces each)
2 tablespoons minced green onion

1 Combine lime juice, soy sauce, ginger, garlic and pepper in medium bowl; mix well. Reserve ¼ cup mixture for serving; set aside. Place salmon in large resealable food storage bag. Pour remaining mixture over salmon; seal bag and turn to coat. Marinate in refrigerator 2 to 4 hours, turning occasionally.

2 Preheat air fryer to 350°F. Line basket with parchment paper or foil; spray lightly with nonstick cooking spray.

3 Cook 8 to 10 minutes or until salmon is lightly crisped and easily flakes when tested with a fork. Brush with reserved marinade mixture; sprinkle with green onion.

CALORIES
440

TOTAL
FAT
27g

CARBS
3g

NET
CARBS
3g

DIETARY
FIBER
0g

PROTEIN
45g

DILL SCROD WITH ASPARAGUS

MAKES 4 SERVINGS

CALORIES
147

TOTAL FAT
2g

CARBS
4g

NET CARBS
2g

DIETARY FIBER
2g

PROTEIN
27g

1 bunch (12 ounces) asparagus spears, ends trimmed

1 teaspoon olive oil

4 scrod or cod fillets (about 5 ounces each)

1 tablespoon lemon juice

1 teaspoon dried dill weed

½ teaspoon salt

¼ teaspoon black pepper

Paprika (optional)

1 Preheat air fryer to 390°F. Line basket with parchment paper or foil; spray lightly with nonstick cooking spray.

2 Drizzle asparagus with oil. Roll asparagus to coat lightly with oil.

3 Drizzle fish with lemon juice. Combine dill weed, salt and pepper in small bowl; sprinkle over fish.

4 Cook 10 to 12 minutes or until fish is opaque in center and begins to flake when tested with a fork. Place fish and asparagus on serving plate. Sprinkle with paprika, if desired.

SIMPLE SALMON WITH FRESH SALSA

MAKES 4 SERVINGS

CALORIES
260

TOTAL FAT
15g

CARBS
7g

NET CARBS
5g

DIETARY FIBER
2g

PROTEIN
25g

4 salmon fillets (about 4 ounces each), rinsed and patted dry
1 teaspoon salt, divided
½ teaspoon dried thyme
¼ teaspoon black pepper
1 medium cucumber, peeled, seeded and chopped
½ large green bell pepper, chopped

½ cup finely chopped radishes
½ cup quartered grape tomatoes
¼ cup chopped fresh cilantro
3 tablespoons fresh lime juice
2 tablespoons finely chopped red onion

1 Preheat air fryer to 350°F. Line basket with parchment paper; spray lightly with nonstick cooking spray. Season salmon with ½ teaspoon salt, thyme and black pepper.

2 Cook 8 to 10 minutes or until salmon is lightly crisped and easily flakes when tested with a fork.

3 Meanwhile, combine cucumber, bell pepper, radishes, tomatoes, cilantro, lime juice, onion and remaining ½ teaspoon salt in medium bowl. Cover; refrigerate until ready to serve.

4 To serve, place salmon on serving plates; top with salsa.

FRESH FISH WITH TOMATOES & HERBS
MAKES 4 SERVINGS

CALORIES
150

TOTAL
FAT
4g

CARBS
4g

NET
CARBS
3g

DIETARY
FIBER
1g

PROTEIN
24g

2 tablespoons plus 2 teaspoons lemon juice, divided

4 white fish fillets (about 1 pound), such as orange roughy or sole

½ teaspoon paprika

1 cup finely chopped seeded tomatoes

2 tablespoons capers, rinsed and drained

2 tablespoons finely chopped fresh parsley

1½ teaspoons dried basil

2 teaspoons olive oil

¼ teaspoon salt

1 Preheat air fryer to 390°F. Line basket with parchment paper or foil; spray lightly with nonstick cooking spray. Drizzle 2 tablespoons lemon juice over fillets; sprinkle with paprika.

2 Cook in batches 8 to 10 minutes or until fish begins to flake when tested with a fork.

3 Meanwhile, in medium saucepan, combine tomatoes, capers, parsley, remaining 2 teaspoons lemon juice, basil, oil and salt. Bring to a boil. Reduce heat and simmer 2 minutes or until hot. Remove from heat.

4 Serve fish topped with tomato mixture.

HALIBUT STEAKS WITH AVOCADO SALSA
MAKES 4 SERVINGS

CALORIES
150

TOTAL
FAT
5g

CARBS
4g

NET
CARBS
2g

DIETARY
FIBER
2g

PROTEIN
22g

4 tablespoons chipotle salsa,
  divided
½ teaspoon salt, divided
4 small (4 to 5 ounces each) *or*
  2 large (8 to 10 ounces each)
  halibut steaks, cut ¾ inch thick

½ cup diced tomato
½ ripe avocado, diced
2 tablespoons chopped fresh
  cilantro (optional)
  Lime wedges (optional)

1 Preheat air fryer to 390°F. Line basket with parchment paper or foil; spray lightly with nonstick cooking spray. Combine 2 tablespoons salsa and ¼ teaspoon salt in small bowl; spread over both sides of halibut.

2 Cook in batches 8 to 10 minutes or until fish is lightly crisped and begins to flake when tested with a fork.

3 Meanwhile, combine remaining 2 tablespoons salsa, ¼ teaspoon salt, tomato, avocado and cilantro, if desired, in small bowl. Mix well and spoon over cooked fish. Garnish with lime wedges.

TUNA TERIYAKI
MAKES 4 SERVINGS

CALORIES 310	

4 fresh tuna steaks
    (about 1½ pounds)*
¼ cup soy sauce
2 tablespoons sake
1½ tablespoons vegetable oil
½ teaspoon minced fresh ginger
¼ teaspoon minced garlic

2 small limes, cut into halves
    Pickled ginger** (optional)

Salmon, halibut or swordfish can be substituted for the tuna.

**Jars of pickled ginger are available in the Asian section of most supermarkets.*

CALORIES
310

TOTAL FAT
14g

CARBS
2g

NET CARBS
2g

DIETARY FIBER
0g

PROTEIN
41g

1 Place tuna in shallow dish. Whisk soy sauce, sake, oil, ginger and garlic in small bowl until smooth. Reserve half of mixture; set aside. Pour remaining half over tuna. Cover and marinate in the refrigerator 40 minutes, turning frequently.

2 Preheat air fryer to 370°F. Line basket with parchment paper or foil; spray lightly with nonstick cooking spray.

3 Cook in batches 12 to 15 minutes or until cooked through.

4 Pour reserved marinade over tuna. Serve with limes and pickled ginger, if desired.

FISH FILLETS IN FRESH CILANTRO CHUTNEY
MAKES 4 SERVINGS

½ cup green onions, cut into ½-inch lengths

1 to 2 hot green chile peppers,* seeded and coarsely chopped

2 tablespoons chopped fresh ginger

2 cloves garlic, peeled

1 cup fresh cilantro leaves

2 tablespoons olive oil

2 tablespoons lime juice

1 teaspoon salt

¼ teaspoon ground cumin

8 large romaine lettuce leaves

4 tilapia or orange roughy fillets (about 1 to 1¼ pounds)

Chile peppers can sting and irritate the skin, so wear rubber gloves when handling peppers and do not touch your eyes.

CALORIES
200

TOTAL FAT
9g

CARBS
7g

NET CARBS
4g

DIETARY FIBER
3g

PROTEIN
24g

1 To prepare chutney, drop green onions, chiles, ginger and garlic through feed tube of food processor with motor running. Stop machine and add cilantro, oil, lime juice, salt and cumin; process until cilantro is finely chopped. Set aside.

2 Trim 1 inch from base of each lettuce leaf; discard. Blanch lettuce leaves in large saucepan of boiling water 30 seconds; remove and drain.

3 Place 2 leaves flat on cutting board, overlapping slightly. Lay one fillet horizontally in center of leaves.

4 Coat each fillet with ¼ of chutney. Fold ends of leaves over fillets; fold top and bottom of leaves over fillets to cover completely.

5 Preheat air fryer to 350°F. Line basket with parchment paper or foil; spray lightly with nonstick cooking spray.

6 Cook 8 to 10 minutes or until fish turns opaque and flakes easily when tested with a fork.

SIDE DISHES

CAULIFLOWER "HASH BROWN" PATTIES
MAKES 8 SERVINGS

CALORIES
90

TOTAL
FAT
4g

CARBS
8g

NET
CARBS
7g

DIETARY
FIBER
1g

PROTEIN
6g

4 slices bacon

1 package (about 12 ounces) cauliflower rice

½ cup finely chopped onion

½ cup finely chopped red and/or green bell pepper

1 large egg

⅓ cup almond flour

½ cup (2 ounces) shredded Cheddar cheese

1 tablespoon chopped fresh chives

1 teaspoon salt

½ teaspoon black pepper

1 Preheat air fryer to 400°F. Cook bacon 8 to 10 minutes. Remove from basket to paper towels; blot any grease from bacon. Crumble into small pieces.

2 Place cauliflower in large bowl. Add bacon, onion, bell pepper, egg, almond flour, cheese, chives, salt and black pepper; mix well. Shape mixture into patties; place on baking sheet. Freeze 30 minutes.

3 Preheat air fryer to 370°F. Line basket with parchment paper or foil; spray lightly with nonstick cooking spray. Cook 12 to 15 minutes or until browned.

BRUSSELS SPROUTS WITH BACON AND BUTTER

MAKES 4 SERVINGS

6 slices thick-cut bacon, cut into ½-inch pieces

1½ pounds Brussels sprouts (about 24 medium), halved

¼ teaspoon salt

¼ teaspoon black pepper

2 tablespoons butter

1 Preheat air fryer to 400°F. Cook bacon 8 to 10 minutes. Remove from basket to paper towels; blot any grease from bacon. Set aside.

2 Preheat air fryer to 390°F. Season Brussels sprouts with salt and pepper.

3 Cook 18 to 20 minutes or until browned, shaking occasionally during cooking. Transfer to large serving bowl; toss with bacon and butter.

CALORIES
220

TOTAL FAT
15g

CARBS
15g

NET CARBS
8g

DIETARY FIBER
7g

PROTEIN
10g

ZUCCHINI TOMATO ROUNDS

MAKES 4 SERVINGS

CALORIES
70

TOTAL
FAT
4g

CARBS
6g

NET
CARBS
4g

DIETARY
FIBER
2g

PROTEIN
2g

2 large zucchini
½ cup cherry tomatoes, sliced
1 tablespoon olive oil

2 cloves garlic, minced
2 teaspoons Italian seasoning
1 teaspoon grated Parmesan cheese

1 Cut zucchini into thin slices three-fourths of the way down (do not cut all the way through). Place zucchini on foil sprayed with nonstick cooking spray.

2 Place tomato slices between each zucchini slice. Combine oil and garlic in small bowl. Drizzle over zucchini. Sprinkle with Italian seasoning and cheese. Wrap foil around zucchini.

3 Preheat air fryer to 390°F. Place foil packets in basket. Cook 10 to 12 minutes or until browned and softened.

"FRIED" CAULIFLOWER FLORETS

MAKES 4 SERVINGS

1 head cauliflower
1 tablespoon olive oil
3 tablespoons grated Parmesan cheese

2 tablespoons almond flour
½ teaspoon salt
½ teaspoon chopped fresh parsley
¼ teaspoon black pepper

1 Cut cauliflower into florets. Place in large bowl. Drizzle with oil. Sprinkle with Parmesan, almond flour, salt, parsley and pepper.

2 Preheat air fryer to 390°F. Spray basket with nonstick cooking spray.

3 Cook in batches 18 to 20 minutes or until browned, shaking every 6 minutes during cooking.

CALORIES
110

TOTAL
FAT
7g

CARBS
8g

NET
CARBS
5g

DIETARY
FIBER
3g

PROTEIN
6g

BROCCOLI ITALIAN STYLE
MAKES 4 SERVINGS

CALORIES
44

TOTAL
FAT
2g

CARBS
7g

NET
CARBS
4g

DIETARY
FIBER
3g

PROTEIN
3g

1¼ pounds fresh broccoli
2 tablespoons lemon juice
1 teaspoon extra virgin olive oil
1 clove garlic, minced

1 teaspoon chopped fresh Italian parsley
Pinch black pepper

1 Trim broccoli, discarding tough stems. Cut broccoli into florets with 2-inch stems. Peel remaining stems; cut into ½-inch slices.

2 Preheat air fryer to 390°F. Spray basket with nonstick cooking spray.

3 Cook in batches 8 to 10 minutes or until tender, shaking occasionally during cooking. Transfer to serving dish.

4 Combine lemon juice, oil, garlic, parsley and pepper in small bowl. Pour over broccoli; toss to coat. Cover and let stand 1 hour before serving to allow flavors to blend. Serve at room temperature.

LEMON CAULIFLOWER

MAKES 6 SERVINGS

CALORIES
106

TOTAL FAT
4g

CARBS
12g

NET CARBS
6g

DIETARY FIBER
6g

PROTEIN
8g

1 tablespoon butter
3 cloves garlic, minced
½ cup water
2 tablespoons lemon juice
4 tablespoons chopped fresh Italian parsley, divided

½ teaspoon grated lemon peel
6 cups (about 1½ pounds) cauliflower florets
¼ cup grated Parmesan cheese
Lemon wedges (optional)

1 Preheat air fryer to 390°F. Line basket with parchment paper or foil; spray lightly with nonstick cooking spray. Heat butter in small saucepan over medium heat. Add garlic; cook and stir 2 to 3 minutes or until soft. Stir in water and lemon juice.

2 Combine garlic mixture, 1 tablespoon parsley, lemon peel and cauliflower in large bowl; toss to blend.

3 Cook in batches 8 to 10 minutes or until tender, shaking occasionally during cooking. Transfer to serving dish. Sprinkle with remaining 3 tablespoons parsley and cheese before serving. Garnish with lemon wedges.

SESAME ASPARAGUS
MAKES 4 SERVINGS

CALORIES
42

TOTAL FAT
2g

CARBS
6g

NET CARBS
3g

DIETARY FIBER
3g

PROTEIN
3g

1 pound medium asparagus spears (about 20), trimmed

1 tablespoon sesame seeds

2 to 3 teaspoons balsamic vinegar

¼ teaspoon salt

¼ teaspoon black pepper

1 Preheat air fryer to 390°F. Line basket with parchment paper or foil; spray lightly with nonstick cooking spray.

2 Spray asparagus lightly with cooking spray. Sprinkle with the sesame seeds, rolling to coat.

3 Cook in batches 8 to 10 minutes or until browned and tender, shaking occasionally during cooking.

4 Remove asparagus to serving dish. Sprinkle with vinegar, salt and pepper.

COOK'S TIP

Be sure to use the entire amount of pepper—it really brings out the flavors of this dish.

SUMMER SQUASH WITH PINE NUTS AND ROMANO CHEESE
MAKES 8 SERVINGS

CALORIES
150

TOTAL
FAT
12g

CARBS
8g

NET
CARBS
6g

DIETARY
FIBER
2g

PROTEIN
4g

3 medium zucchini, cut into ½-inch slices

3 medium summer squash, cut into ½-inch slices

1 medium red bell pepper, chopped

½ cup chopped yellow onion

1 clove garlic, minced

½ cup chopped pine nuts

⅓ cup grated Romano cheese

1 teaspoon Italian seasoning

1 teaspoon salt

¼ teaspoon black pepper

1 tablespoon unsalted butter, cubed

1 Preheat air fryer to 370°F. Line basket with parchment paper or foil; spray lightly with nonstick cooking spray. Combine zucchini, summer squash, bell pepper, onion and garlic in basket; toss to blend.

2 Combine pine nuts, cheese, Italian seasoning, salt and black pepper in small bowl; stir to blend. Fold cheese mixture into squash. Dot mixture with butter.

3 Cook 10 to 12 minutes or until vegetables are heated through and cheese mixture is golden brown.

ASPARAGUS WITH GOAT CHEESE SAUCE
MAKES 4 SERVINGS

1 pound asparagus, trimmed

1 package (3½ ounces) goat cheese

¾ cup chicken broth

¼ cup dry white wine

2 cloves garlic, minced

2 tablespoons chopped fresh chives

1 Preheat air fryer to 390°F. Spray basket with nonstick cooking spray.

2 Cook in batches 8 to 10 minutes or until tender, shaking occasionally during cooking.

3 Meanwhile, mash cheese in medium nonstick skillet; stir in broth, wine and garlic. Simmer over medium heat 8 to 10 minutes or until desired thickness, stirring frequently. Fold in chives; serve immediately over asparagus.

CALORIES
135

TOTAL FAT
8g

CARBS
7g

NET CARBS
5g

DIETARY FIBER
2g

PROTEIN
8g

OKRA AND TOMATOES

MAKES 8 SERVINGS

CALORIES
50

TOTAL
FAT
2g

CARBS
9g

NET
CARBS
6g

DIETARY
FIBER
3g

PROTEIN
2g

1 package (16 ounces) cut frozen okra, thawed

1 can (about 14 ounces) diced tomatoes, undrained

1 medium onion, chopped

½ large green bell pepper, chopped

1 stalk celery, chopped

1 tablespoon olive oil

1 clove minced garlic

¾ teaspoon salt

½ teaspoon dried basil

½ teaspoon dried oregano

½ teaspoon black pepper

1 Preheat air fryer to 370°F. Line basket with parchment paper or foil; spray lightly with nonstick cooking spray.

2 Combine okra, tomatoes, onion, bell pepper, celery, oil, garlic, salt, basil, oregano and black pepper in large bowl; toss to blend.

3 Cook in batches 5 to 7 minutes or until heated through.

DILLED BRUSSELS SPROUTS

MAKES 4 SERVINGS

CALORIES
60

TOTAL
FAT
4g

CARBS
6g

NET
CARBS
3g

DIETARY
FIBER
3g

PROTEIN
3g

1 package (10 ounces) frozen Brussels sprouts *or* 1 pint fresh Brussels sprouts

1 tablespoon olive oil

1 teaspoon dried dill weed

1 teaspoon dried minced onion

Salt and black pepper

1 Preheat air fryer to 390°F. Combine Brussels sprouts with oil, dill weed and onion in large bowl; toss to coat.

2 Cook 15 to 18 minutes or until golden browned, shaking occasionally during cooking. Season with salt and pepper.

METRIC CONVERSION CHART

VOLUME MEASUREMENTS (dry)

$\frac{1}{8}$ teaspoon = 0.5 mL
$\frac{1}{4}$ teaspoon = 1 mL
$\frac{1}{2}$ teaspoon = 2 mL
$\frac{3}{4}$ teaspoon = 4 mL
1 teaspoon = 5 mL
1 tablespoon = 15 mL
2 tablespoons = 30 mL
$\frac{1}{4}$ cup = 60 mL
$\frac{1}{3}$ cup = 75 mL
$\frac{1}{2}$ cup = 125 mL
$\frac{2}{3}$ cup = 150 mL
$\frac{3}{4}$ cup = 175 mL
1 cup = 250 mL
2 cups = 1 pint = 500 mL
3 cups = 750 mL
4 cups = 1 quart = 1 L

VOLUME MEASUREMENTS (fluid)

1 fluid ounce (2 tablespoons) = 30 mL
4 fluid ounces ($\frac{1}{2}$ cup) = 125 mL
8 fluid ounces (1 cup) = 250 mL
12 fluid ounces (1$\frac{1}{2}$ cups) = 375 mL
16 fluid ounces (2 cups) = 500 mL

WEIGHTS (mass)

$\frac{1}{2}$ ounce = 15 g
1 ounce = 30 g
3 ounces = 90 g
4 ounces = 120 g
8 ounces = 225 g
10 ounces = 285 g
12 ounces = 360 g
16 ounces = 1 pound = 450 g

DIMENSIONS

$\frac{1}{16}$ inch = 2 mm
$\frac{1}{8}$ inch = 3 mm
$\frac{1}{4}$ inch = 6 mm
$\frac{1}{2}$ inch = 1.5 cm
$\frac{3}{4}$ inch = 2 cm
1 inch = 2.5 cm

OVEN TEMPERATURES

250°F = 120°C
275°F = 140°C
300°F = 150°C
325°F = 160°C
350°F = 180°C
375°F = 190°C
400°F = 200°C
425°F = 220°C
450°F = 230°C

BAKING PAN SIZES

Utensil	Size in Inches/Quarts	Metric Volume	Size in Centimeters
Baking or Cake Pan (square or rectangular)	8×8×2	2 L	20×20×5
	9×9×2	2.5 L	23×23×5
	12×8×2	3 L	30×20×5
	13×9×2	3.5 L	33×23×5
Loaf Pan	8×4×3	1.5 L	20×10×7
	9×5×3	2 L	23×13×7
Round Layer Cake Pan	8×1½	1.2 L	20×4
	9×1½	1.5 L	23×4
Pie Plate	8×1¼	750 mL	20×3
	9×1¼	1 L	23×3
Baking Dish or Casserole	1 quart	1 L	—
	1½ quart	1.5 L	—
	2 quart	2 L	—